Tenth Workshop on Building and Using Comparable Corpora 2017

Held at ACL 2017

Vancouver, Canada
3 August 2017

ISBN: 978-1-5108-4575-6

ACL 2017

Tenth Workshop on
Building and Using Comparable Corpora

Proceedings of the Workshop

August 3, 2017
Vancouver, Canada

Introduction

In the language engineering and the linguistics communities, research on comparable corpora has been motivated by two main reasons. In language engineering, on the one hand, it is chiefly motivated by the need to use comparable corpora as training data for statistical Natural Language Processing applications such as statistical machine translation or cross-lingual retrieval. In linguistics, on the other hand, comparable corpora are of interest in themselves by making possible inter-linguistic discoveries and comparisons. It is generally accepted in both communities that comparable corpora are documents in one or several languages that are comparable in content and form in various degrees and dimensions. We believe that the linguistic definitions and observations related to comparable corpora can improve methods to mine such corpora for applications of statistical NLP. As such, it is of great interest to bring together builders and users of such corpora.

Comparable corpora are collections of documents that are comparable in content and form in various degrees and dimensions. This definition includes many types of parallel and non-parallel multilingual corpora, but also sets of monolingual corpora that are used for comparative purposes. Research on comparable corpora is active but used to be scattered among many workshops and conferences. The workshop series on "Building and Using Comparable Corpora" (BUCC) aims at promoting progress in this exciting emerging field by bundling its research, thereby making it more visible and giving it a better platform.

Following the nine previous editions of the workshop which took place in Africa (LREC'08 in Marrakech), North America (ACL'11 in Portland), Asia (ACL-IJCNLP'09 in Singapore and ACL-IJCNLP'15 in Beijing), Europe (LREC'10 in Malta, ACL'13 in Sofia, and LREC'14 in Reykjavik) and also on the border between Asia and Europe (LREC'12 in Istanbul), the workshop this year has returned to North America, first time in Canada in Vancouver.

We would like to thank all people who in one way or another helped in making this workshop once again a success. Our special thanks go to Philippe Langlais for accepting to give the keynote talk, to the members of the program committee who did an excellent job in reviewing the submitted papers under strict time constraints, and to the ACL'17 workshop chairs and organizers. Last but not least we would like to thank our authors and the participants of the workshop.

This year the workshop included a shared task to quantitatively evaluate competing methods for extracting parallel sentences from comparable monolingual corpora, so as to give an overview on the state of the art and to identify the best performing approaches. 13 runs were submitted in time to the shared task by 4 teams, covering three of the four proposed language pairs: French-English (7 runs), German-English (3 runs), and Chinese-English (3 runs). We make the datasets are available on the workshop Web page at `https://comparable.limsi.fr/bucc2017/bucc2017-task.html`.

Serge Sharoff, Pierre Zweigenbaum, Reinhard Rapp   August 2017

Organizers:

Serge Sharoff	University of Leeds, UK
Pierre Zweigenbaum	LIMSI, CNRS, Université Paris-Saclay, Orsay, France
Reinhard Rapp	Magdeburg-Stendal University of Applied Sciences and University of Mainz, Germany

Program Committee:

Ahmet Aker	University of Sheffield, UK
Hervé Déjean	Xerox Research Centre Europe, Grenoble, France
Kurt Eberle	Lingenio, Germany
Andreas Eisele	European Commission, Luxembourg
Éric Gaussier	Université Joseph Fourier, Grenoble, France
Vishal Goyal	Punjabi University, Patiala, India
Silvia Hansen-Schirra	University of Mainz, Germany
Hitoshi Isahara	Toyohashi University of Technology
Kyo Kageura	University of Tokyo, Japan
Philippe Langlais	Université de Montrèal, Canada
Shervin Malmasi	Harvard Medical School, Boston, MA, USA
Michael Mohler	Language Computer Corp., US
Emmanuel Morin	Université de Nantes, France
Dragos Stefan Munteanu	Language Weaver, Inc., US
Ted Pedersen	University of Minnesota, Duluth, US
Reinhard Rapp	Magdeburg-Stendal University of Applied Sciences and University of Mainz, Germany
Serge Sharoff	University of Leeds, UK
Michel Simard	National Research Council Canada
Pierre Zweigenbaum	LIMSI-CNRS, Orsay, France

Invited Speaker:

Philippe Langlais, Université de Montrèal, Canada

Table of Contents

Workshop Program

9:00 - 9:05	**Opening**
9:05 - 10:00	**Invited presentation**

Users and Data: The Two Neglected Children of Bilingual Natural Language Processing Research
Phillippe Langlais

Session 1: **Plagiarism detection**
10:00 - 10:30 *Deep Investigation of Cross-Language Plagiarism Detection Methods*
Jérémy Ferrero, Laurent Besacier, Didier Schwab and Frédéric Agnès

10:30 - 11:00 **Coffee break**

Session 2: **Sentence alignment and lexicon acquisition**
11:00 - 11:30 *Sentence Alignment using Unfolding Recursive Autoencoders*
Jeenu Grover and Pabitra Mitra
11:30 - 12:00 *Acquisition of Translation Lexicons for Historically Unwritten Languages via Bridging Loanwords*
Michael Bloodgood and Benjamin Strauss

12:00 - 14:00 **Lunch**

Session 3: **Building comparable corpora**
14:00 - 14:30 *Toward a Comparable Corpus of Latvian, Russian and English Tweets*
Dmitrijs Milajevs
14:30 - 15:00 *Automatic Extraction of Parallel Speech Corpora from Dubbed Movies*
Alp Öktem, Mireia Farrús and Leo Wanner
15:00 - 15:30 *A parallel collection of clinical trials in Portuguese and English*
Mariana Neves

15:30 - 16:00 **Coffee break**

Session 4: **Shared task session**
16:00 - 16:20 *Overview on the Second BUCC Shared Task: Spotting Parallel Sentences in Comparable Corpora*
Pierre Zweigenbaum, Serge Sharoff, Reinhard Rapp
16:20 - 16:40 *Weighted Set-Theoretic Alignment of Comparable Sentences*
Andoni Azpeitia, Thierry Etchegoyhen and Eva Martínez Garcia
16:40 - 17:00 *BUCC 2017 Shared Task: a First Attempt Toward a Deep Learning Framework for Identifying Parallel Sentences in Comparable Corpora*
Francis Grégoire and Philippe Langlais
17:00 - 17:20 *zNLP: Identifying Parallel Sentences in Chinese-English Comparable Corpora*
Zheng Zhang and Pierre Zweigenbaum
17:20 - 17:40 *BUCC2017: A Hybrid Approach for Identifying Parallel Sentences in Comparable Corpora*
Sainik Mahata, Dipankar Das and Sivaji Bandyopadhyay

17:40 - 17:50 **Closing**

Users and Data: The Two Neglected Children
of Bilingual Natural Language Processing Research

Philippe Langlais
RALI-DIRO
Université de Montréal
CP. 6128 Succ. Centre Ville
H3C 3J7 Montréal, Québec, Canada
`felipe@iro.umontreal.ca`

Abstract

Despite numerous studies devoted to mining parallel material from bilingual data, we have yet to see the resulting technologies wholeheartedly adopted by professional translators and terminologists alike. I argue that this state of affairs is mainly due to two factors: the emphasis published authors put on models (even though data is as important), and the conspicuous lack of concern for actual end-users.

1 Introduction

Parallel corpora (documents collections that are translations of one another) are the bread and butter of machine translation (MT). Solutions have been proposed for mining parallel texts found on the Web (Chen and Nie, 2000; Resnik and Smith, 2003), and for aligning sentences in parallel documents (Gale and Church, 1993), leading to so-called "bitexts". It then becomes possible to align words in parallel sentence pairs, in an unsupervised way (Brown et al., 1993).

Because parallel data is relatively rare, researchers have turned to exploiting comparable corpora, e.g. news articles in different languages covering the same event. Sharoff et al. (2013) thoroughly examine this topic. It is noteworthy that researchers know quite well how to identify parallel sentences in a comparable corpus (Munteanu and Marcu, 2005), and can then use "tried and true" procedures for extracting bilingual lexicons from such a resource (Rapp, 1995; Fung, 1995; Mikolov et al., 2013).

Being able to benefit from both parallel and comparable data is quite an accomplishment from a scientific point of view, and progress is still being made on the task. In contrast, and frustratingly, the technologies that professional translators are adopting continue to rely mainly on sentence-based translation memories. I do not mean to say that other technologies are not being used. For instance, translation agencies are increasingly integrating machine translation into their workflow, but this is mostly driven by cost reduction, and not by a genuine interest in MT on the part of translators, who remain unconvinced.

I submit that this limited adoption of new resources and technologies is due to the conjunction of two factors: the overall lack of concern for actual users, and the clear preference of the research community for the study of models at the cost of research on data. Of course, improvements on models have the potential to impact users. Notably, recent studies (Bentivogli et al., 2016; Isabelle et al., 2017) confirm that neural MT (Sutskever et al., 2014; Cho et al., 2014; Bahdanau et al., 2014) significantly reduces errors, therefore requiring less post-editing. However, better ways of efficiently acquiring and organizing data equally matters.

As for end-users, more interest in their day-to-day concerns should lead to a better adoption of the technologies we develop, which in turn would reveal scientific challenges we had never thought of before. One example of a project I have been involved in is the (at that time pioneering) effort to develop an interactive translation engine named TransType (Foster et al., 1997) in which a translator interacts iteratively with a translation engine in order to produce a translation. After multiple rounds of development, we had several translators beta-test our prototype (Langlais et al., 2002), and we realized that the keystroke saving rate used to measure the improvements brought about by TransType was *not* correlated with the user's productivity gains. This led us to devise a user model that we could not have foreseen at the beginning of the project (Foster et al., 2002). See (González-

1

Proceedings of the 10th Workshop on Building and Using Comparable Corpora, pages 1–5,
Vancouver, Canada, August 3, 2017. ©2017 Association for Computational Linguistics

Rubio et al., 2012) for further developments along these lines.

Doing research in a vacuum certainly facilitates progress. For instance, in recent years we have witnessed a tremendous interest in embedding methods for extracting bilingual lexicons, thanks to the pioneering work of (Mikolov et al., 2013). It is nowadays a standard procedure to measure the quality of embedding representations on what is called the bilingual lexicon induction (BIL) task. One popular evaluation protocol, initially proposed in (Mikolov et al., 2013) consists in identifying the translation of the last 1000 words of the 6000 most frequent words in the training material. However, for many language pairs of interest, existing bilingual lexicons already list the translations of frequent (and less frequent) words. In fact, in (Jakubina and Langlais, 2017), we show that the accuracy of embedding-based methods when translating rare words — which arguably is a test case of better use to end users — is less than 2% at rank 1. I must make it clear at this point that I am excited by embedding methods and their potential to improve the current state of the art. I am merely saying that the way we evaluate these methods does not reflect their true usefulness.

The purpose of this presentation is to pinpoint a number of challenges I feel are worth being reinvestigated. They belong to two categories: understanding better how to acquire and organize (bilingual) data, and better exploiting existing resources, with an emphasis on more representative test cases. This list is not exhaustive, and emanates from the needs expressed by some of the industry professionals I have been discussing with, and from the opinions I have been forming over time when reading (exciting) publications in my field.

2   Overlooked Issues

2.1   Data Acquisition

Finding parallel documents over the Web has been studied early by (Chen and Nie, 2000; Resnik and Smith, 2003). Those systems (and others like them) perform resource alignment by examining their URLs. Since this superficial information is sometimes misleading, they also use other features such as length ratios, lexicon overlap or HTML structure mapping. As noted in (Buck and Koehn, 2016), efforts in gathering parallel data have been mostly ad-hoc and limited in scale. I believe these limitations stem precisely from the fact that we are more concerned by models than data in the academia. Interestingly, the bilingual alignment document shared task at WMT 2016 is a very sensible attempt to promote research to find solutions to the aforementioned problem. I hope this is a rallying first step, fostering a new interest in striking a compromise between efficiency and effectiveness, in the spirit of (Ture et al., 2011).

Conventional wisdom tells us that parallel data is (comparatively) rare, therefore there is a need for mining comparable corpora. Munteanu and Marcu (2005) show that cross-lingual information retrieval coupled with a filter on the publication date of the news offer an efficient way of gathering comparable news data over the Web. Smith et al. (2010) demonstrate that language inter-linked article pairs in Wikipedia offer valuable comparable data. Still, I am not aware of any large-scale and systematic way of **mining comparable data over the Web**.

Gathering **domain-specific bilingual corpora** (parallel and comparable) is a related issue that has many practical benefits, but which I feel is neglected. Compiling domain-specific monolingual data is difficult enough (Groc and Tannier, 2014), in a multilingual setting, it is even more complex to begin to agree on best practices. See (Azoulay, 2017) for a recent attempt and (Morin et al., 2010) for evidences that the quantity of texts acquired should not be the only concern.

2.2   Data Organization

Large-scale acquisition efforts conducted over the Web involve at some point an effort to distinguish parallel data from comparable or even unrelated data. A similar situation arises in institutions that produce documents in multiple languages without necessarily keeping track of which documents are parallel or comparable, and with what level of quality. A typical example of this are news agencies.

The classification of (Fung and Cheung, 2004) is very useful to qualify the kind of bilingual data we are dealing with, as are measures of the comparability of a corpus (Li and Gaussier, 2010; Babych and Hartley, 2014). I think more efforts should be invested in **estimating the quality of a bilingual corpus** (parallel or comparable). It could prove useful for instance when choosing the appropriate extraction technique for a given pair of documents. For example, we could select a monotonous sentence-alignment if the documents are near-parallel, and Cartesian product-based approaches if the documents are merely comparable.

Produced texts are increasingly becoming multilingual, through various processes that are not all known. While the overused parliamentary Hansard debates are created by a well-known process, for many collections, the **genesis of a document** is simply not known. This poses exciting challenges that have been partially addressed, among which detecting that a text has been produced by translation (whether it be automatic or not) (Carter and Inkpen, 2012; Arase and Zhou, 2013). This feature might impact applications such as plagiarism detection (Ceska et al., 2008).

2.3 Parallel Material Extraction

Having a collection of parallel and comparable corpora available allows for extracting translation units. Sentences have been the focus of much research, and we know rather well how to align sentences in a parallel corpus. While aligning legislative texts and the like is more or less a solved problem (Langlais et al., 1998), **aligning literary texts** is still very challenging (Xu et al., 2015). Goutte et al. (2012) report that statistical MT is robust with respect to noise in sentence alignment. At the same time, Lamraoui and Langlais (2013) show that carefully aligning sentences in a collection as well structured as Europarl (Koehn, 2005) leads to (slight) increases in performance. These somehow contradictory results warrant further investigations.

At the other end of the spectrum of units, we typically seek to align words. So-called IBM models (Brown et al., 1993) are popular generative models that can be learnt in order to extract word pairs in parallel data. Still, **identifying multiword expressions and their translations** remains an actively studied[1] and challenging task. In particular, Isabelle et al. (2017) have observed that idioms are poorly handled by neural machine translation.

Aligning units in a comparable corpus remains a challenge as well. Recognizing sentences that are translations of one another in a comparable corpus has been studied early by (Munteanu and Marcu, 2005), but advances in **embedding methods** might improve the current state of the art. We have participated in this year's BUCC shared task on parallel sentence extraction from compara-

---

[1]The MWE workshop is at its 13th edition.

ble corpora with such an approach (Grégoire and Langlais, 2017), and I expect this research avenue to gain in popularity. With the exception of (Kumano and Tokunaga, 2007) and (Quirk et al., 2007), we lack a **generative model of a comparable corpus** that would allow to capture parts of documents that are aligned in a principled way, whatever the granularity (paragraphs, sentences, expressions, words or even subwords).

For progress in extraction to be meaningful, we should pay attention to the way we measure it: Not all units are equally important. For instance, pairs of compositional units are not worth being collected (and therefore evaluated). Likewise, mining sentence pairs in which n-grams have already been seen massively is likely not very helpful. We believe that the community should share a number of benchmarks that are representative of specific uses. Ultimately, this should involve users because they know best what matters to them.

3 Discussion

Progress in acquiring bilingual collections of texts, organizing them into a meaningful repository, and extracting knowledge from it are three avenues that are clearly overlapping. Many of those aspects have received attention by many researchers, and have been the focus of dedicated projects, such as ACCURAT (Skadia et al., 2010).

Still, our (or at least my) understanding of how to efficiently mine bilingual material for a specific use is deficient. I believe one reason for this is that our community is more versed in elaborating models and evaluating them in a vacuum, whereas I think data is definitely part of the game, and we should work on better ways of evaluating our technology. This presentation will be punctuated by a number of studies conducted at RALI, some of which involve real-life users.

References

Yuki Arase and Ming Zhou. 2013. Machine translation detection from monolingual web-text. In *51st Annual Meeting of the Association for Computational Linguistics*. Sofia, Bulgaria, pages 1597–1607.

Daphnée Azoulay. 2017. Frame-based knowledge representation using large specialized corpora. In *AAAI Spring Symposium on Computational Construction Grammar and Natural Language Understanding*. Stanford University, CA, pages 119–226.

Bogdan Babych and Anthony Hartley. 2014. Meta-evaluation of comparability metrics using parallel corpora. *CoRR* abs/1404.3759.

Dzmitry Bahdanau, Kyunghyun Cho, and Yoshua Bengio. 2014. Neural machine translation by jointly learning to align and translate. In *ICLR 2015*.

Luisa Bentivogli, Arianna Bisazza, Mauro Cettolo, and Marcello Federico. 2016. Neural versus phrase-based machine translation quality: a case study. *CoRR* abs/1608.04631.

Peter F. Brown, Stephen A. Della Pietra, Vincent J. Della Pietra, and Robert L. Mercer. 1993. The mathematics of statistical machine translation. *Computational Linguistics* 19(2):263–313.

Christian Buck and Philipp Koehn. 2016. Findings of the WMT 2016 Bilingual Document Alignment Shared Task. In *Proceedings of the First Conference on Machine Translation*. pages 554–563.

Dave Carter and Diana Inkpen. 2012. Searching for poor quality machine translated text : learning the difference between human writing and machine translations. In *25th Canadian Conference on Artificial Intelligence*. Toronto, Canada, pages 49–60.

Zdenek Ceska, Michal Toman, and Karel Jezek. 2008. Multilingual plagiarism detection. In *Proceedings of the 13th International Conference on Artificial Intelligence: Methodology, Systems, and Applications*. AIMSA '08, pages 83–92.

Jiang Chen and Jian-Yun Nie. 2000. Parallel web text mining for cross-language ir. In *Content-Based Multimedia Information Access - Volume 1*. RIAO '00, pages 62–77.

Kyunghyun Cho, Bart van Merriënboer, Çalar Gülçehre, Dzmitry Bahdanau, Fethi Bougares, Holger Schwenk, and Yoshua Bengio. 2014. Learning phrase representations using rnn encoder–decoder for statistical machine translation. In *Proceedings of the 2014 Conference on Empirical Methods in Natural Language Processing*. pages 1724–1734.

George Foster, Pierre Isabelle, and Pierre Plamondon. 1997. Target-text mediated interactive machine translation. *Machine Translation* 12(1):175–194.

George Foster, Philippe Langlais, and Guy Lapalme. 2002. User-friendly text prediction for translators. In *Empirical Methods in Natural Language Processing*. Philadelphia.

Pascale Fung. 1995. Compiling bilingual lexicon entries from a non-parallel english-chinese corpus. In *3rd Workshop on Very Large Corpora*. pages 173–183.

Pascale Fung and Percy Cheung. 2004. Multi-level bootstrapping for extracting parallel sentences from a quasi-comparable corpus. In *Proceedings of the 20th international conference on Computational Linguistics*.

William A. Gale and Kenneth W. Church. 1993. A program for aligning sentences in bilingual corpora. *Computational linguistics* 19(1):75102.

Jesús González-Rubio, Daniel Ortiz-Martínez, and Francisco Casacuberta. 2012. Active learning for interactive machine translation. In *13th Conference of the European Chapter of the Association for Computational Linguistics*. pages 245–254.

Cyril Goutte, Marine Carpuat, and George Foster. 2012. The impact of sentence alignment errors on phrase-based machine translation performance. In *10th AMTA*.

Françis Grégoire and Philippe Langlais. 2017. Bucc 2017 shared task: a first attempt toward a deep learning framework for identifying parallel sentences in comparable corpora. In *BUCC Workshop*. Vancouver, Canada. Shared task paper.

Clément De Groc and Xavier Tannier. 2014. Evaluating Web-as-corpus Topical Document Retrieval with an Index of the OpenDirectory. In *Proceedings of the 9th International Conference on Language Resources and Evaluation (LREC 2014)*. Reykjavk, Iceland.

P. Isabelle, C. Cherry, and G. Foster. 2017. A Challenge Set Approach to Evaluating Machine Translation. *ArXiv e-prints* .

Laurent Jakubina and Philippe Langlais. 2017. Reranking translation candidates produced by several bilingual word similarity sources. In *15th Conference of the European Chapter of the Association for Computational Linguitics*. volume 2, Short Papers, pages 605–611.

Philipp Koehn. 2005. Europarl: A Parallel Corpus for Statistical Machine Translation. In *tenth Machine Translation Summit*. pages 79–86.

Tadashi Kumano and Hideki Tanaka Takenobu Tokunaga. 2007. Extracting phrasal alignments from comparable corpora by using joint probability smt model. In *11th International Conference on Theoretical and Methodological Issues in Machine Translation*.

Fethi Lamraoui and Philippe Langlais. 2013. Yet another fast, robust and open source sentence aligner. time to reconsider sentence alignment? In *XIV Machine Translation Summit*. Nice, France, pages 77–84.

Philippe Langlais, Guy Lapalme, and Marie Loranger. 2002. Transtype: Development-Evaluation Cycles to Boost Translators' Productivity. *Machine Translation, Kluwer Academic Publishers*, 17:77–98.

Philippe Langlais, Michel Simard, and Jean Véronis. 1998. Methods and Practical Issues in Evaluating Alignment Techniques. In *36th Annual Meeting of the Association for Computational Linguistics (ACL) and 17th International Conference on Computational Linguistic (COLING)*. Montreal, Canada.

Bo Li and Éric Gaussier. 2010. Improving corpus comparability for bilingual lexicon extraction from comparable corpora. In *Proceedings of the 23rd International Conference on Computational Linguistics.* page 644652.

Tomas Mikolov, Quoc V. Le, and Ilya Sutskever. 2013. Exploiting similarities among languages for machine translation. *arXiv preprint arXiv:1309.4168* .

Emmanuel Morin, Béatrice Daille, Kyo Kageura, and Koichi Takeuchi. 2010. Brains, not Brawn: The Use of 'Smart" Comparable Corpora in Bilingual Terminology Mining. *ACM Transactions on Speech and Language Processing* 7(1):1–23.

Dragos S. Munteanu and Daniel Marcu. 2005. Improving machine translation performance by exploiting non-parallel corpora. *Computational Linguistics* 31(4):477504.

Chris Quirk, Raghavendra Udupa, and Arul Menezes. 2007. Generative models of noisy translations with applications to parallel fragment extraction. In *In Proceedings of MT Summit XI, European Association for Machine Translation.*

Reinhard Rapp. 1995. Identifying word translations in non-parallel texts. In *Proceedings of the 33rd annual meeting on Association for Computational Linguistics.* pages 320–322.

Philip Resnik and Noah A. Smith. 2003. The web as a parallel corpus. *Computational Linguistics* 29(3):349380.

Serge Sharoff, Reinhard Rapp, and Pierre Zweigenbaum. 2013. *Overviewing Important Aspects of the Last Twenty Years of Research in Comparable Corpora*, Springer, pages 1–17.

Inguna Skadia, Andrejs Vasijevs, Raivis Skadi, Robert Gaizauskas, and Dan Tufi. 2010. Analysis and evaluation of comparable corpora for under resourced areas of machine translation. In *Proceedings of the 3rd Workshop on Building and Using Comparable Corpora. Applications of Parallel and Comparable Corpora in Natural Language Engineering and the Humanities.* pages 6–14.

Jason R. Smith, Chris Quirk, and Kristina Toutanova. 2010. Extracting parallel sentences from comparable corpora using document level alignment. In *Human Language Technologies: The 2010 Annual Conference of the North American Chapter of the Association for Computational Linguistics.* page 403411.

Ilya Sutskever, Oriol Vinyals, and Quoc V. Le. 2014. Sequence to sequence learning with neural networks. In *Proceedings of the 27th International Conference on Neural Information Processing Systems.* pages 3104–3112.

Ferhan Ture, Tamer Elsayed, and Jimmy Lin. 2011. No free lunch: brute force vs. locality-sensitive hashing for cross-lingual pairwise similarity. In *Proceedings of the 34th international ACM SIGIR conference on Research and development in Information Retrieval.* pages 943–952.

Yong Xu, Aurlien Max, and François Yvon. 2015. Sentence alignment for literary texts. *Linguistic Issues in Language Technology* 12(6):1–29.

Deep Investigation of Cross-Language Plagiarism Detection Methods

Jérémy Ferrero
Compilatio
276 rue du Mont Blanc
74540 Saint-Félix, France
LIG-GETALP
Univ. Grenoble Alpes, France
jeremy.ferrero@imag.fr

Laurent Besacier
LIG-GETALP
Univ. Grenoble Alpes, France
laurent.besacier@imag.fr

Didier Schwab
LIG-GETALP
Univ. Grenoble Alpes, France
didier.schwab@imag.fr

Frédéric Agnès
Compilatio
276 rue du Mont Blanc
74540 Saint-Félix, France
frederic@compilatio.net

Abstract

This paper is a deep investigation of cross-language plagiarism detection methods on a new recently introduced open dataset, which contains parallel and comparable collections of documents with multiple characteristics (different genres, languages and sizes of texts). We investigate cross-language plagiarism detection methods for 6 language pairs on 2 granularities of text units in order to draw robust conclusions on the best methods while deeply analyzing correlations across document styles and languages.

1 Introduction

Plagiarism is a very significant problem nowadays, specifically in higher education institutions. In monolingual context, this problem is rather well treated by several recent researches (Potthast et al., 2014). Nevertheless, the expansion of the Internet, which facilitates access to documents throughout the world and to increasingly efficient (freely available) machine translation tools, helps to spread *cross-language plagiarism*. Cross-language plagiarism means plagiarism by translation, *i.e.* a text has been plagiarized while being translated (manually or automatically). The challenge in detecting this kind of plagiarism is that the suspicious document is no longer in the same language of its source. In this relatively new field of research, no systematic evaluation of the main

methods, on several language pairs, for different text granularities and for different text genres, has been proposed yet. This is what we propose in this paper.

Contribution. The paper focus is on cross-language semantic textual similarity detection which is the main part (with source retrieval) in cross-language plagiarism detection. The evaluation dataset used (Ferrero et al., 2016) allows us to run a large amount of experiments and analyses. To our knowledge, this is the first time that full potential of such a diverse dataset is used for benchmarking. So, the paper main contribution is a systematic evaluation of cross-language similarity detection methods (using in plagiarism detection) on different languages, sizes and genres of texts through a reproducible evaluation protocol. Robust conclusions are derived on the best methods while deeply analyzing correlations across document styles and languages. Due to space limitations, we only provide a subset of our experiments in the paper while more result tables and correlation analyses are provided as supplementary material on a Web link[1].

Outline. After presenting the dataset used for our study in section 2, and reviewing the state-of-the-art methods of cross-language plagiarism detection that we evaluate in section 3, we describe the evaluation protocol employed in section 4. Then, section 5.1 presents the correla-

---

[1] https://github.com/FerreroJeremy/
Cross-Language-Dataset/tree/master/study

Proceedings of the 10th Workshop on Building and Using Comparable Corpora, pages 6–15,
Vancouver, Canada, August 3, 2017. ©2017 Association for Computational Linguistics

tion of the methods across language pairs, while section 5.2 presents a detailed analysis on only English-French pair. Finally, section 6 concludes this work and gives a few perspectives.

2 Dataset

The reference dataset used during our study is the new dataset[2] recently introduced by Ferrero et al. (2016). The dataset was specially designed for a rigorous evaluation of cross-language textual similarity detection. The different characteristics of the dataset are synthesized in Table 1, while Table 2 presents the number of aligned units by subcorpus and by granularity.

More precisely, the characteristics of the dataset are the following:

- it is multilingual: it contains French, English and Spanish texts;

- it proposes cross-language alignment information at different granularities: document level, sentence level and chunk level;

- it is based on both parallel and comparable corpora (mix of Wikipedia, scientific conference papers, amazon product reviews, Europarl and JRC);

- it contains both human and machine translated texts;

- it contains different percentages of named entities;

- part of it has been obfuscated (to make the cross-language similarity detection more complicated) while the rest remains without noise;

- the documents were written and translated by multiple types of authors (from average to professionals);

- it covers various fields.

3 Overview of State-of-the-Art Methods

Textual similarity detection methods are not exactly methods to detect plagiarism. Plagiarism is a statement that someone copied text deliberately without attribution, while these methods only detect textual similarities. There is no way

---

of knowing why texts are similar and thus to assimilate these similarities to plagiarism.

At the moment, there are five classes of approaches for cross-language plagiarism detection. The aim of each method is to estimate if two textual units in different languages express the same message or not. Figure 1 presents a taxonomy of Potthast et al. (2011), enriched by the study of Danilova (2013), of the different cross-language plagiarism detection methods grouped by class of approaches. We only describe below the state-of-the-art methods that we evaluate in the paper, one for each class of approaches (those in bold in the Figure 1).

Cross-Language Character N-Gram (CL-CnG) is based on Mcnamee and Mayfield (2004) model. We use the *CL-C3G* Potthast et al. (2011)'s implementation. Only spaces and alphanumeric characters are kept. Any other diacritic or symbol is deleted and the texts are lower-cased. The texts are then segmented into 3-grams (sequences of 3 contiguous characters) and transformed into *tf.idf* vectors of character 3-grams. The metric used to compare two vectors is the cosine similarity.

Cross-Language Conceptual Thesaurus-based Similarity (CL-CTS) aims to measure the semantic similarity using abstract concepts from words in textual units. We reuse the idea of Pataki (2012) which, for each sentence, build a bag-of-words by getting all the available translations of each word of the sentence. For that, we use a linked lexical resource called *DBNary* (Sérasset, 2015). The bag-of-words of a sentence is the merge of the bag-of-words of the words of the sentence. After, we use the Jaccard distance (Jaccard, 1912) with fuzzy matching between two bag-of-words to measure the similarity between two sentences.

Cross-Language Alignment-based Similarity Analysis (CL-ASA) was introduced for the first time by Barrón-Cedeño et al. (2008) and developed subsequently by Pinto et al. (2009). The model aims to determinate how a textual unit is potentially the translation of another textual unit using bilingual unigram dictionary which contains translations pairs (and their probabilities) extracted from a parallel corpus. Our lexical dictionary is calculated applying the IBM-1 model

Sub-corpus	Alignment	Authors	Translations	Obfuscation	NE (%)
JRC-Acquis	Parallel	Politicians	Professional translators	No	3.74
Europarl	Parallel	Politicians	Professional translators	No	7.74
Wikipedia	Comparable	Average people	-	Noise	8.37
PAN (Gutenberg Project)	Parallel	Professional authors	Professional authors	Yes	3.24
Amazon Product Reviews	Parallel	Average people	Google Translate	Noise	6.04
Conference papers	Comparable	NLP scientists	NLP scientists	Noise	9.36

Table 1: Characteristics of the dataset (Ferrero et al., 2016) for each sub-corpus. The percentages of named entities (NE) present in the last column are estimated with Stanford Named Entity Recognizer[3].

Sub-corpus	Languages	# Documents	# Sentences	# Noun chunks
JRC-Acquis	EN, FR, ES	$\simeq$ 10,000	$\simeq$ 150,000	$\simeq$ 10,000
Europarl	EN, FR, ES	$\simeq$ 10,000	$\simeq$ 475,000	$\simeq$ 25,600
Wikipedia	EN, FR, ES	$\simeq$ 10,000	$\simeq$ 5,000	$\simeq$ 150
PAN (Gutenberg Project)	EN, ES	$\simeq$ 3,000	$\simeq$ 90,000	$\simeq$ 1,400
Amazon Product Reviews	EN, FR	$\simeq$ 6,000	$\simeq$ 23,000	$\simeq$ 2,600
Conference papers	EN, FR	$\simeq$ 35	$\simeq$ 1,300	$\simeq$ 300

Table 2: Number of aligned documents, sentences and noun chunks by sub-corpus.

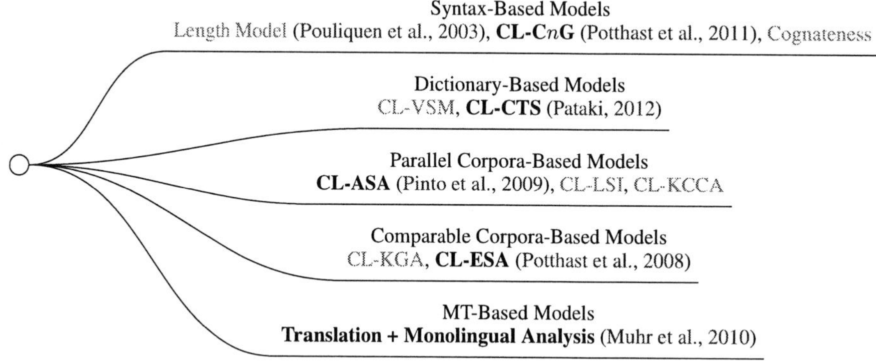

Figure 1: Taxonomy of Potthast et al. (2011), enriched by the study of Danilova (2013), of different approaches for cross-language similarity detection.

(Brown et al., 1993) on the concatenation of TED[4] (Cettolo et al., 2012) and News[5] parallel corpora. We reuse the implementation of Pinto et al. (2009) that proposed a formula that factored the alignment function.

Cross-Language Explicit Semantic Analysis (CL-ESA) is based on the explicit semantic analysis model introduced for the first time by Gabrilovich and Markovitch (2007), which represents the meaning of a document by a vector based on the vocabulary derived from Wikipedia, to find a document within a corpus. It was reused by Potthast et al. (2008) in the context of cross-language

document retrieval. Our implementation uses a part of Wikipedia, from which our test data was removed, to build the vector representations of the texts.

Translation + Monolingual Analysis (T+MA) consists in translating suspect plagiarized text back into the same language of source text, in order to operate a monolingual comparison between them. We use the Muhr et al. (2010)'s implementation which consists in replacing each word of one text by its most likely translations in the language of the other text, leading to a bags-of-words. We use *DBNary* (Sérasset, 2015) to get the translations. The metric used to compare two texts is a monolingual matching based on strict intersection of bags-of-words.

---

[3] http://nlp.stanford.edu/software/CRF-NER.shtml

[4] https://wit3.fbk.eu/

[5] http://www.statmt.org/wmt13/translation-task.html#download

More recently, SemEval-2016 (Agirre et al., 2016) proposed a new subtask on evaluation of cross-lingual semantic textual similarity. Despite the fact that it was the first year that this subtask was attempted, there were 26 submissions from 10 teams. Most of the submissions relied on a machine translation step followed by a monolingual semantic similarity, but 4 teams tried to use learned vector representations (on words or sentences) combined with machine translation confidence (for instance the submission of Lo et al. (2016) or Ataman et al. (2016)). The method that achieved the best performance (Brychcin and Svoboda, 2016) was a supervised system built on a word alignment-based method proposed by Sultan et al. (2015). This very recent method is, however, not evaluated in this paper.

4 Evaluation Protocol

We apply the same evaluation protocol as in Ferrero et al. (2016)'s paper. We build a distance matrix of size N x M, with $M = 1,000$ and $N = |S|$ where S is the evaluated sub-corpus. Each textual unit of S is compared to itself (actually, since this is cross-lingual similarity detection, each source language unit is compared to its corresponding unit in the target language) and to M-1 other units randomly selected from S. The same unit may be selected several times. Then, a matching score for each comparison performed is obtained, leading to the distance matrix. Thresholding on the matrix is applied to find the threshold giving the best F_1 score. The F_1 score is the harmonic mean of precision and recall. Precision is defined as the proportion of relevant matches (similar cross-language units) retrieved among all the matches retrieved. Recall is the proportion of relevant matches retrieved among all the relevant matches to retrieve. Each method is applied on each sub-corpus for chunk and sentence granularities. For each configuration (*i.e.* a particular method applied on a particular sub-corpus considering a particular granularity), 10 folds are carried out by changing the M selected units.

5 Investigation of Cross-Language Similarity Performances

5.1 Across Language Pairs

Table 3 brings together the performances of all methods on all sub-corpora for each pair of languages at *chunk* and *sentence* level. In both sub-tables, at chunk and sentence level, the overall F_1 score over all sub-corpora of one method in one particular language pair is given.

As a preliminary remark, one should note that *CL-C3G* and *CL-ESA* lead to the same results for a given language pair (same performance if we reverse source and target languages) due to their symmetrical property. Another remark we can make is that methods are consistent across language pairs: best performing methods are mostly the same, whatever the language pair considered. This is confirmed by the calculation of the Pearson correlation between performances of different pairs of languages, from Table 3 and reported in Table 4. Table 4 represents the Pearson correlations between the different language pairs of the overall results of all methods on all sub-corpora. This result is interesting because some of these methods depend on the availability of lexical resources whose quality is heterogeneous across languages. Despite the variation of the source and target languages, a minimum Pearson correlation of 0.940 for EN→FR vs. FR→ES, and a maximum of 0.998 for EN→FR vs. EN→ES and ES→FR vs. FR→ES at chunk level is observed (see Table 4). For the sentence granularity, it is the same order of magnitude: the maximum Pearson correlation is 0.997 for ES→EN vs. EN→ES and ES→FR vs. FR→ES, and the minimum is 0.913 for EN→ES vs. FR→ES (see Table 4). In average the language pair EN→FR is 0.975 correlated with the other language pairs (0.980 at chunk-level and 0.971 at sentence-level), for instance. This correlation suggests the possibility to tune a method on one language and apply it to another language if needed.

Table 5 synthesizes the top 3 methods for each language pair observed in Tables 3 and 4. No matter the source and target languages or the granularity, *CL-C3G* generally outperforms the other methods. Then *CL-ASA*, *CL-CTS* and *T+MA* are also closely efficient but their behavior depends on the granularity. Generally, *CL-ASA* is better at the chunk granularity, followed by *CL-CTS* and *T+MA*. On the contrary, *CL-CTS* and *T+MA* are slightly more effective at sentence granularity. One explanation for this is that *T+MA* depends on the quality of machine translation, which may have poor performance on isolated chunks, while a short length text unit benefits the *CL-CTS* and *CL-ASA* methods because of their formula which

Chunk level						
Methods	**EN→FR**	**FR→EN**	**EN→ES**	**ES→EN**	**ES→FR**	**FR→ES**
CL-C3G	**0.5071**	**0.5071**	**0.4375**	**0.4375**	**0.4795**	**0.4795**
CL-CTS	0.4250	04116	0.3780	0.3881	0.4203	0.4169
CL-ASA	0.4738	0.4252	0.4083	0.3941	0.3736	0.3540
CL-ESA	0.1499	0.1499	0.1476	0.1476	0.1520	0.1520
T+MA	0.3730	0.3634	0.3177	0.3279	0.3158	0.3140
Sentence level						
Methods	**EN→FR**	**FR→EN**	**EN→ES**	**ES→EN**	**ES→FR**	**FR→ES**
CL-C3G	**0.4931**	**0.4931**	**0.3819**	**0.3819**	0.4577	**0.4577**
CL-CTS	0.4734	0.4633	0.3171	0.3204	**0.4645**	0.4575
CL-ASA	0.3576	0.3523	0.2694	0.2531	0.3098	0.2843
CL-ESA	0.1430	0.1430	0.1337	0.1337	0.1383	0.1383
T+MA	0.3760	0.3692	0.3505	0.3526	0.3673	0.3525

Table 3: Overall F_1 score over all sub-corpora of the state-of-the-art methods for each language pair (EN: English; FR: French; ES: Spanish).

Chunk level							
EN→FR	**FR→EN**	**EN→ES**	**ES→EN**	**ES→FR**	**FR→ES**	**Overall**	**Lang. Pair**
1.000	0.991	**0.998**	0.995	0.957	0.940	0.980	**EN→FR**
	1.000	0.990	0.994	0.980	0.971	0.987	**FR→EN**
		1.000	0.996	0.967	0.949	0.983	**EN→ES**
			1.000	0.978	0.965	0.988	**ES→EN**
				1.000	**0.998**	0.980	**ES→FR**
					1.000	0.970	**FR→ES**

Sentence level							
EN→FR	**FR→EN**	**EN→ES**	**ES→EN**	**ES→FR**	**FR→ES**	**Overall**	**Lang. Pair**
1.000	1.000	0.929	0.922	0.991	0.982	0.971	**EN→FR**
	1.000	0.931	0.924	0.989	0.981	0.971	**FR→EN**
		1.000	**0.997**	0.925	0.913	0.949	**EN→ES**
			1.000	0.928	0.922	0.949	**ES→EN**
				1.000	**0.997**	0.971	**ES→FR**
					1.000	0.966	**FR→ES**

Table 4: Pearson correlations of the overall F_1 score over all sub-corpora of all methods between the different language pairs (EN: English; FR: French; ES: Spanish).

will tend to minimize the number of false positives in this case. Anyway, despite these differences in ranking, the gap in term of performance values is small between these closest methods. For instance, we can see that when *CL-CTS* is more efficient than *CL-C3G* (ES→FR column at sentence level in Table 3 and Table 5 (b)), the difference of performance is very small (0.0068).

Table 6 shows the Pearson correlations of the results (of all methods on all sub-corpora) by language pair between the chunk and the sentence granularity (correlations calculated from Table 3, between the EN→FR column at chunk level with the EN→FR column at sentence level, and so on). We can see a strong Pearson correlation of the performances on the language pair between the chunk and the sentence granularity (an average of 0.9, with 0.907 for the EN→FR pair, for instance). This proves that all methods behave along a simi-

EN↔FR	ES↔FR
EN↔ES	
CL-C3G	CL-C3G
CL-ASA	CL-CTS
CL-CTS	CL-ASA

(a) Chunk granularity

EN↔FR	EN↔ES	ES→FR
FR→ES		
CL-C3G	CL-C3G	CL-CTS
CL-CTS	T+MA	CL-C3G
T+MA	CL CTS	T+MA

(b) Sentence granularity

Table 5: Top 3 methods by source and target language.

lar trend at chunk and at sentence level, regardless of the languages on which they are used. However, we can see in Table 7 that if we collect correlation scores separately for each method (on all sub-corpora, on all language pairs) between chunk

Chunk level					
Methods	**Wikipedia (%)**	**TALN (%)**	**JRC (%)**	**APR (%)**	**Europarl (%)**	**Overall (%)**
CL-C3G	62.91 ± 0.815	40.90 ± 0.500	36.63 ± 0.826	80.30 ± 0.703	53.29 ± 0.583	50.71 ± 0.655
CL-CTS	58.00 ± 0.519	33.71 ± 0.382	29.87 ± 0.815	67.51 ± 1.050	44.95 ± 1.157	42.50 ± 1.053
CL-ASA	23.33 ± 0.724	23.39 ± 0.432	33.14 ± 0.936	26.49 ± 1.205	55.50 ± 0.681	47.38 ± 0.781
CL-ESA	64.89 ± 0.664	23.78 ± 0.613	14.03 ± 0.997	23.14 ± 0.777	14.19 ± 0.590	14.99 ± 0.709
T+MA	58.22 ± 0.756	39.13 ± 0.551	28.61 ± 0.597	73.14 ± 0.666	36.95 ± 1.502	37.30 ± 1.200
Sentence level					
Methods	**Wikipedia (%)**	**TALN (%)**	**JRC (%)**	**APR (%)**	**Europarl (%)**	**Overall (%)**
CL-C3G	48.25 ± 0.349	48.08 ± 0.538	36.68 ± 0.693	61.10 ± 0.581	52.72 ± 0.866	49.31 ± 0.798
CL-CTS	46.68 ± 0.437	38.67 ± 0.552	28.21 ± 0.612	50.82 ± 1.034	53.21 ± 0.601	47.34 ± 0.632
CL-ASA	27.63 ± 0.330	27.25 ± 0.341	35.17 ± 0.644	25.53 ± 0.795	36.55 ± 1.139	35.76 ± 0.978
CL-ESA	51.14 ± 0.875	14.25 ± 0.334	14.44 ± 0.341	13.93 ± 0.714	13.91 ± 0.618	14.30 ± 0.551
T+MA	50.57 ± 0.888	37.79 ± 0.364	32.36 ± 0.369	61.94 ± 0.756	37.92 ± 0.552	37.60 ± 0.518

Table 8: Average F_1 scores and confidence intervals of methods applied on EN→FR sub-corpora at chunk and sentence level – 10 folds validation.

Lang. Pair	**Correlation**
EN→FR	0.907
FR→EN	0.946
EN→ES	0.833
ES→EN	0.838
ES→FR	0.932
FR→ES	0.939

Table 6: Pearson correlations of the results of all methods on all sub-corpora, between the chunk and the sentence granularity, by language pair (EN: English; FR: French; ES: Spanish) (calculated from Table 3).

Methods	**Correlation**
CL-C3G	0.996
CL-CTS	0.970
CL-ASA	0.649
CL-ESA	0.515
T+MA	0.780

Table 7: Pearson correlations of the results on all sub-corpora on all language pairs, between the chunk and the sentence granularity, by methods (calculated from Table 3).

and sentence granularity performances (correlations also calculated from Table 3, between the *CL-C3G* line at chunk level with the *CL-C3G* line at sentence level, and so on), we notice that some methods exhibit a different behavior at both chunk and sentence granularities: for instance, this is the case for *CL-ASA* which seems to be really better at chunk level. In conclusion, we can say that the methods presented here may behave slightly differently depending on the text unit considered (chunk or sentence) but they behave practically the same no matter the languages of the compared texts are (as long as enough lexical resources are available for dealing with these languages).

5.2 Detailed Analysis for English-French

The previous sub-section has shown a consistent behavior of methods across language pairs (strongly consistent) and granularities (less strongly consistent). For this reason, we now propose a detailed analysis for different sub-corpora, *for the English-French language pair - at chunk and sentence level - only*. Providing these results for all language pairs and granularities would take too much space. Moreover, we also run those state-of-the-art methods on the dataset of the Spanish-English cross-lingual Semantic Textual Similarity task of SemEval-2016 (Agirre et al., 2016) and SemEval-2017 (Cer et al., 2017), and propose a shallower but equally rigorous analysis. However, all those results are also made available as supplementary material on our paper Web page.

Table 8 shows the performances of methods on the EN→FR sub-corpora. As mentioned earlier, *CL-C3G* is in general the most effective method. *CL-ESA* seems to show better results on comparable corpora, like Wikipedia. In contrast, *CL-ASA* obtains better results on parallel corpora such as JRC or Europarl collections. *CL-CTS* and *T+MA* are pretty efficient and versatile too. It is also interesting to note that the results of the methods are well correlated between certain types of sub-corpora. For instance, the Pearson correlation of the performances of all methods between the TALN sub-corpus and the APR sub-corpus, is 0.982 at the chunk level, and 0.937 at the sentence level. This means that a method could be optimized on a particular corpus (for instance APR) and applied efficiently on another corpus (for instance TALN which is made of scientific conference papers).

11

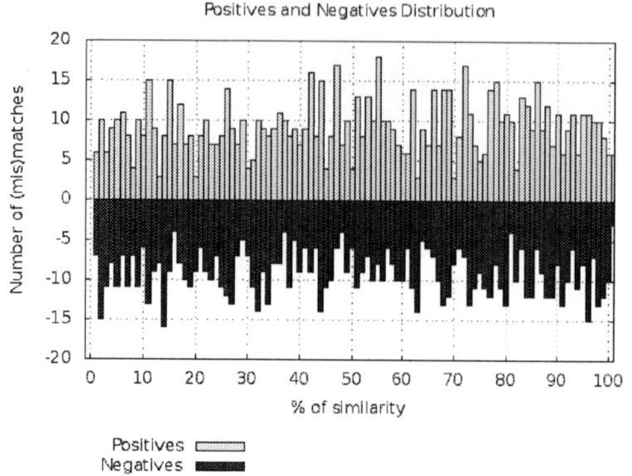

(a) Distribution histogram (fingerprint) of a random distribution.

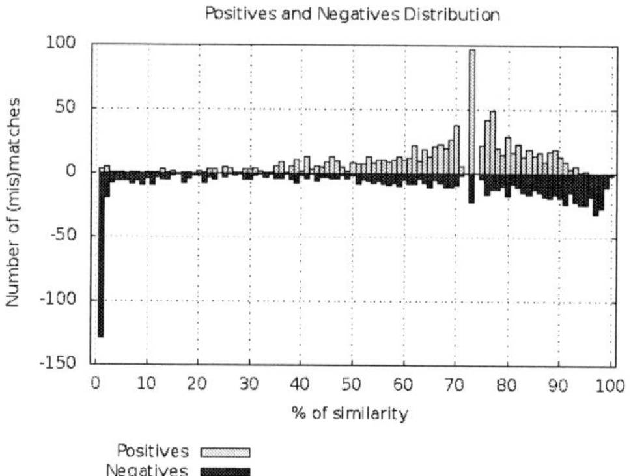

(b) Distribution histogram (fingerprint) of the *Length Model* of Pouliquen et al. (2003).

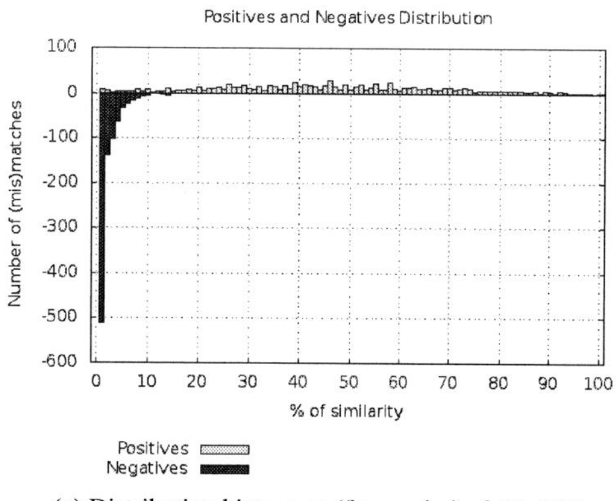

(c) Distribution histogram (fingerprint) of *CL-C3G*.

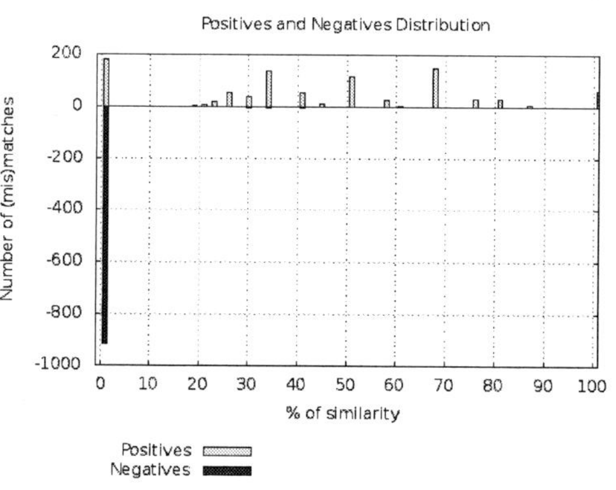

(d) Distribution histogram (fingerprint) of *CL-CTS*.

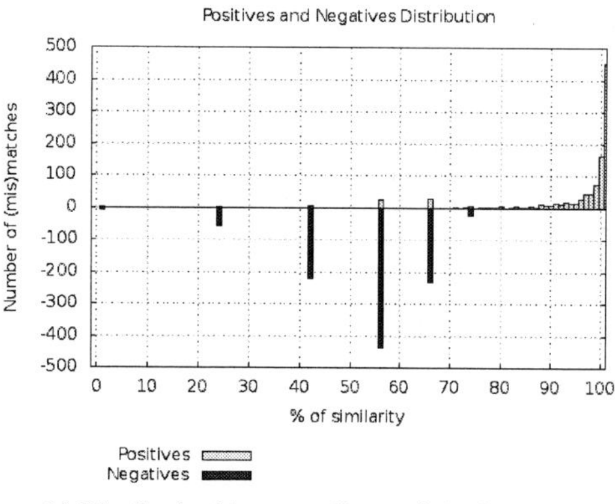

(e) Distribution histogram (fingerprint) of *CL-ASA*.

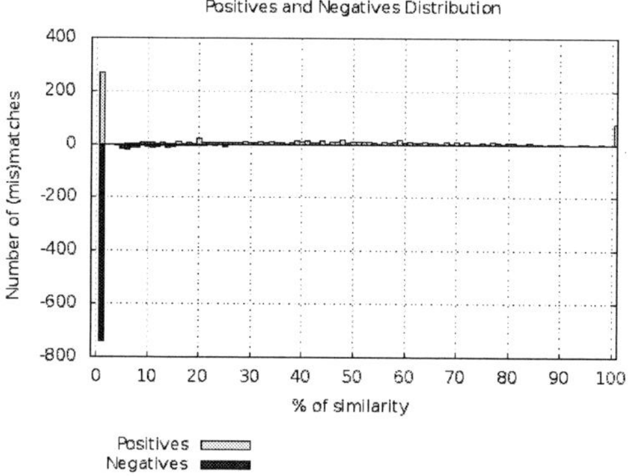

(f) Distribution histogram (fingerprint) of *T+MA*.

Figure 2: Distribution histograms of some state-of-the-art methods for 1000 positives and 1000 negatives (mis)matches. X-axis represents the similarity score (in percentage) computed by the method, and Y-axis represents the number of (mis)matches found for a given similarity score. In white, in the upper part of the figures, the positives (units that needed to be matched), and in black, in the lower part, the negatives (units that should not be matched).

Beyond their capacity to correctly predict a (mis)match, an interesting feature of the methods is their clustering capacity, *i.e.* their ability to cor- rectly separate the positives (cross-lingual seman- tic textual similar units) and the negatives (textual units with different meaning) in order to minimize

Methods	T	P	R	F_1
Random baseline	0.003	0.501	0.999	0.668
Length Model	0.203	0.566	0.970	0.714
CL-C3G	0.087	0.972	0.953	0.962
CL-CTS	0.010	0.986	0.808	0.888
CL-ASA	0.762	0.937	0.772	0.847
T+MA	0.157	0.928	0.646	0.762

Table 9: Precision (P), Recall (R) and F_1 score, reached at a certain threshold (T), of some state-of-the-art methods for a data subset made with 1000 positives and 1000 negatives (mis)matches – 10 folds validation.

the doubts on the classification. To verify this phenomenon, we conducted another experience with a new protocol. We built a data subset by concatenating some documents of the previously presented dataset (Ferrero et al., 2016). More precisely we used 200 pairs of each sub-corpora at sentence level only. We compared 1000 English textual units to their corresponding unit in French, and to one other (not relevant) French unit. So, each English textual unit must strictly leads to one match and one mismatch, *i.e.* in the end, we have exactly 1000 matches and 1000 mismatches for a run. We repeat this experiment 10 times for each method, leading to 10 folds for each method.

The results of this experiment are reported on Table 9, that shows the average for the 10 folds of the Precision (P), the Recall (R) and the F_1 score of some state-of-the-art methods, reached at a certain threshold (T). The results are also reported in Figure 2, in the form of distribution histograms of the evaluated methods for 1000 positives and 1000 negatives (mis)matches. X-axis represents the similarity score (in percentage) computed by the method, and Y-axis represents the number of (mis)matches found for a given similarity score. In white, in the upper part of the figures, the positives (units that needed to be matched), and in black, in the lower part, the negatives (units that should not be matched).

Distribution histograms on Figure 2 highlights the fact that each method has its own fingerprint: even if two methods looks equivalent in term of performances (see Table 9), their clustering capacity, and so the distribution of their (mis)matches can be different. For instance, we can see that a random distribution is a very bad distribution (Figure 2 (a)). We can also see that *CL-C3G* has a narrow distribution of negatives and a broad distribution for positives (Figure 2 (c)), whereas

the opposite is true for *CL-ASA* (Figure 2 (e)). Table 9 confirms this phenomenon by the fact that the decision threshold is very different for *CL-ASA* (0.762) compared to the other methods (around 0.1). This means that *CL-ASA* discriminates more correctly the positives that the negatives, when it seems to be the opposite for the other methods. For this reason, we can make the assumption that some methods are complementary, due to their different *fingerprint*. These behaviors suggest that fusion between these methods (notably decision tree based fusion) should lead to very promising results.

6 Conclusion

We conducted a deep investigation of cross-language plagiarism detection methods on a challenging dataset. Our results have shown a common behavior of methods across different language pairs. We revealed strong correlations across languages but also across text units considered. This means that when a method is more effective than another on a sufficiently large dataset, it is generally more effective in any other case. This also means that if a method is efficient on a particular language pair, it will be similarly efficient on another language pair as long as enough lexical resources are available for these languages.

We also investigated the behavior of the methods through the different types of texts on a particular language pair: English-French. We revealed strong correlations across types of texts. This means that a method could be optimized on a particular corpus and applied efficiently on another corpus.

Finally, we have shown that methods behave differently in clustering match and mismatched units, even if they seem similar in performance. This opens new possibilities for their combination or fusion.

More results supporting these facts are provided as supplementary material[6].

References

Eneko Agirre, Carmen Banea, Daniel Cer, Mona Diab, Aitor Gonzalez-Agirre, Rada Mihalcea, and Janyce Wiebe. 2016. SemEval-2016 Task 1: Semantic Textual Similarity, Monolingual and Cross-Lingual Evaluation. In *Proceedings of the 10th In-*

---

[6]https://github.com/FerreroJeremy/Cross-Language-Dataset/tree/master/study

ternational Workshop on Semantic Evaluation (SemEval 2016). San Diego, CA, USA, pages 497–511. http://www.aclweb.org/anthology/S16-1081.

Duygu Ataman, Jose G. C. de Souza, Marco Turchi, and Matteo Negri. 2016. FBK HLT-MT at SemEval-2016 Task 1: Cross-lingual semantic similarity measurement using quality estimation features and compositional bilingual word embeddings. In *Proceedings of the 10th International Workshop on Semantic Evaluation (SemEval 2016)*. San Diego, CA, USA, pages 570–576. https://www.aclweb.org/anthology/S/S16/S16-1086.pdf.

Alberto Barrón-Cedeño, Paolo Rosso, David Pinto, and Alfons Juan. 2008. On Cross-lingual Plagiarism Analysis using a Statistical Model. In Benno Stein and Efstathios Stamatatos and Moshe Koppel, editor, *Proceedings of the ECAI'08 PAN Workshop: Uncovering Plagiarism, Authorship and Social Software Misuse*. Patras, Greece, pages 9–13.

Peter F. Brown, Vincent J. Della Pietra, Stephen A. Della Pietra, and Robert L. Mercer. 1993. The Mathematics of Statistical Machine Translation: Parameter Estimation. *Computational Linguistics* 19(2):263–311. http://www.aclweb.org/anthology/J93-2003.

Tomas Brychcin and Lukas Svoboda. 2016. UWB at SemEval-2016 Task 1: Semantic textual similarity using lexical, syntactic, and semantic information. In *Proceedings of the 10th International Workshop on Semantic Evaluation (SemEval 2016)*. San Diego, CA, USA, pages 588–594. https://www.aclweb.org/anthology/S/S16/S16-1089.pdf.

Daniel Cer, Mona Diab, Eneko Agirre, Inigo Lopez-Gazpio, and Lucia Specia. 2017. Semeval-2017 task 1: Semantic textual similarity multilingual and crosslingual focused evaluation. In *Proceedings of the 11th International Workshop on Semantic Evaluation (SemEval-2017)*. Association for Computational Linguistics, Vancouver, Canada, pages 1–14. http://www.aclweb.org/anthology/S17-2001.

Mauro Cettolo, Christian Girardi, and Marcello Federico. 2012. Wit^3: Web inventory of transcribed and translated talks. In *Proceedings of the 16th Conference of the European Association for Machine Translation (EAMT)*. pages 261–268.

Vera Danilova. 2013. Cross-Language Plagiarism Detection Methods. In Galia Angelova, Kalina Bontcheva, and Ruslan Mitkov, editors, *Proceedings of the Student Research Workshop associated with RANLP 2013*. Hissar, Bulgaria, Recent Advances in Natural Language Processing, pages 51–57. http://aclweb.org/anthology/R/R13/R13-2008.pdf.

Jérémy Ferrero, Frédéric Agnès, Laurent Besacier, and Didier Schwab. 2016. A Multilingual, Multi style and Multi-granularity Dataset for Cross-language Textual Similarity Detection. In *Proceedings of the Tenth International Conference on Language Resources and Evaluation (LREC'16)*. European Language Resources Association (ELRA), Portoroz, Slovenia, pages 4162–4169. ISLRN: 723-785-513-738-2. http://islrn.org/resources/723-785-513-738-2/.

Evgeniy Gabrilovich and Shaul Markovitch. 2007. Computing Semantic Relatedness using Wikipedia-based Explicit Semantic Analysis. In *Proceedings of the 20th International Joint Conference on Artifical Intelligence (IJCAI'07)*. Morgan Kaufmann Publishers Inc., Hyderabad, India, pages 1606–1611.

Paul Jaccard. 1912. The distribution of the flora in the alpine zone. *New Phytologist* 11(2):37–50. https://doi.org/10.1111/j.1469-8137.1912.tb05611.x.

Chi-kiu Lo, Cyril Goutte, and Michel Simard. 2016. CNRC at SemEval-2016 Task 1: Experiments in crosslingual semantic textual similarity. In *Proceedings of the 10th International Workshop on Semantic Evaluation (SemEval 2016)*. San Diego, CA, USA, pages 668–673. http://www.aclweb.org/anthology/S/S16-1102.pdf.

Paul Mcnamee and James Mayfield. 2004. Character N-Gram Tokenization for European Language Text Retrieval. *Information Retrieval Proceedings* 7(1-2):73–97.

Markus Muhr, Roman Kern, Mario Zechner, and Michael Granitzer. 2010. External and Intrinsic Plagiarism Detection Using a Cross-Lingual Retrieval and Segmentation System - Lab Report for PAN at CLEF 2010. In Martin Braschler, Donna Harman, and Emanuele Pianta, editors, *CLEF Notebook*. Padua, Italy.

Màté Pataki. 2012. A New Approach for Searching Translated Plagiarism. In *Proceedings of the 5th International Plagiarism Conference*. Newcastle, UK, pages 49–64.

David Pinto, Jorge Civera, Alfons Juan, Paolo Rosso, and Alberto Barrón-Cedeño. 2009. A Statistical Approach to Crosslingual Natural Language Tasks. *Journal of Algorithms* 64(1):51–60. https://doi.org/10.1016/j.jalgor.2009.02.005.

Martin Potthast, Alberto Barrón-Cedeño, Benno Stein, and Paolo Rosso. 2011. Cross-Language Plagiarism Detection. *Language Resources and Evaluation* 45(1):45–62. https://doi.org/10.1007/s10579-009-9114-z.

Martin Potthast, Matthias Hagen, Anna Beyer, Matthias Busse, Martin Tippmann, Paolo Rosso, and Benno Stein. 2014. Overview of the 6th International Competition on Plagiarism Detection. In *PAN at CLEF 2014*. Sheffield, UK, pages 845–876.

Martin Potthast, Benno Stein, and Maik Anderka.
2008. A Wikipedia-Based Multilingual Retrieval
Model. In *30th European Conference on IR Research (ECIR'08)*. Springer, Glasgow, Scotland, volume 4956 of *LNCS of Lecture Notes in Computer Science*, pages 522–530.

Bruno Pouliquen, Ralf Steinberger, and Camelia Ignat.
2003. Automatic Identification of Document Translations in Large Multilingual Document Collections.
In *Proceedings of the International Conference Recent Advances in Natural Language Processing (RANLP'03)*. Borovets, Bulgaria, pages 401–408.

Gilles Sérasset. 2015. DBnary: Wiktionary as
a Lemon-Based Multilingual Lexical Resource in
RDF. *Semantic Web Journal (special issue on Multilingual Linked Open Data)* 6(4):355–361.
https://doi.org/10.3233/SW-140147.

Md Arafat Sultan, Steven Bethard, and Tamara
Sumner. 2015. DLS@CU: Sentence similarity from word alignment and semantic vector
composition. In *Proceedings of the 9th International Workshop on Semantic Evaluation (SemEval 2015)*. Denver, CO, USA, pages 148–153.
http://www.aclweb.org/anthology/S15-2027.

Sentence Alignment using Unfolding Recursive Autoencoders

Jeenu Grover
IIT Kharagpur
India - 721302
groverjeenu@gmail.com

Pabitra Mitra
IIT Kharagpur
India - 721302
pabitra@cse.iitkgp.ernet.in

Abstract

In this paper, we propose a novel two step algorithm for sentence alignment in monolingual corpora using Unfolding Recursive Autoencoders. First, we use *unfolding recursive auto-encoders* (RAE) to learn feature vectors for phrases in syntactical tree of the sentence. To compare two sentences we use a similarity matrix which has dimensions proportional to the size of the two sentences. Since the similarity matrix generated to compare two sentences has varying dimension due to different sentence lengths, a dynamic pooling layer is used to map it to a matrix of fixed dimension. The resulting matrix is used to calculate the similarity scores between the two sentences. The second step of the algorithm captures the contexts in which the sentences occur in the document by using a dynamic programming algorithm for global alignment.

1 Introduction

Neural Network based architectures are increasingly being used for capturing the semantics of the Natural Language (Pennington et al., 2014). We put them to use for alignment of the sentences in monolingual corpora. Sentence alignment can be formally defined as a mapping of sentences from one document to other such that a sentence pair belongs to the mapping iff both the sentences convey the same semantics in their respective texts. The mapping can be many-to-many as a sentence(s) in one document could be split into multiple sentences in the other to convey same information. It is to be noted that this task is different form paraphrase identification because here we are not just considering the similarity between two individual sentences but we are also considering the context in a sense that we are making use of the order in which the sentences occur in documents.

Text alignment in Machine Translation (MT) tasks varies a lot from sentence alignment in monolingual corpora as MT tasks deal with bilingual corpora which exhibits a very strong level of alignment. But two comparable documents in monolingual corpora, such as two articles written about a common entity or two newspaper reports about an event, use widely divergent forms to express same information content. They may contain paraphrases, alternate wording, change of sentence and paragraph order etc. As a result, the surface-based techniques which rely on comparing the sentence lengths, sentence ordering etc. are less likely to be useful for monolingual sentence alignment as opposed to their effectiveness in alignment of bilingual corpora.

Sentence alignment finds its use in applications such as plagiarism detection(Clough et al., 2002), information retrieval and question answering(Marsi and Krahmer, 2005). It can also be used to generate training set data for tasks such as text summarization.

2 Related Work

A lot of work has been done on the problem of sentence alignment which relies on the surface properties of the text in natural language such as word overlap(Hatzivassiloglou et al., 2001; Barzilay and Elhadad, 2003), bag-of-words model(Nelken and Shieber, 2006). It relies mainly in the field of statistical machine learning (Barzilay and Elhadad, 2003). A little has been done to improve upon this task by capturing the semantics of the text.

Barzilay and Elhadad show that a similarity measure combined with contextual information outperforms methods based on sentence similar-

Proceedings of the 10th Workshop on Building and Using Comparable Corpora, pages 16–20,
Vancouver, Canada, August 3, 2017. ©2017 Association for Computational Linguistics

ity functions. Nelken and Shieber improved upon the sentence similarity function by borrowing TF-IDF based scoring from the information retrieval literature and outperformed all other methods.

Their work can be summarized in 4 steps:

1. TF*IDF : Treat each sentence as a document and compute it's TF*IDF vector. For a word t in sentence[1] s, $TF_s(t)$ denotes the number of times t occurs in s, **N** is the number of sentences in document and $DF(t)$ indicates the occurrences of t in document.

$$w_s(t) = Tf_s(t) \times \log \frac{N}{DF(t)} \qquad (1)$$

where $w_s(t)$, denotes the value for dimension corresponding to word t in TF-IDF vector of sentence s.

2. The previous step gave the similarity measure of 2 sentences. It was converted to an appropriate probability measure denoting the $Pr(align(s_i, s_j) = 1)$ by using logistic regression on the training data.

3. Heuristic Alignment : They simply choose sentence pairs between two documents with $pr(align) > th$, where th is the threshold. Additionally heuristics such as mapping the first sentences of two documents (as justified by Quirk et al.(Dolan et al., 2004)) and allowing 2-to-1 mapping of adjacent sentences are followed.

4. Global Alignment with Dynamic Programming: They compute the optimal alignment between sentences 1..i of one text and sentences 1..j of the elementary version by using a dynamic programming approach similar to Needleman and Wunsch (1970).

3 Approach

In this section, we briefly visit the neural network models and other techniques that would be used in our task.

3.1 Neural Embeddings

The idea of using neural embeddings is to get **n**-dimensional space representations for the words in vocabulary **V**. We define a mapping

$$\mathbf{L_w} : \mathbf{V} \to \mathbb{R}^\mathbf{n} \qquad (2)$$

---

[1]We are using terms "word" and "sentence" in their literal sense and not according to the TF-IDF terminology.

which embeds words into a semantic vector space where the metric approximates semantic similarity. The idea of neural embeddings was first introduced by Bengio et al.(2003) and later worked upon by Turian et al.(2010). Mikolov et al.(2013) points that the words with similar meaning are mapped closer in this new feature space. The directions in the vector space correspond to different semantic concepts.

Turian et al.(2010) gave us an encoding from a given word to a vector in the semantic space. Now, we want to have an embedding from a sentence to a vector in the semantic space, i.e. given,

$$\mathbf{L_w} : \mathbf{V} \to \mathbb{R}^\mathbf{n} \qquad (3)$$

we want to get,

$$\mathbf{L_s} : \mathbf{V}^* \to \mathbb{R}^\mathbf{n} \qquad (4)$$

To get such a mapping, we use autoencoders recursively on the parse tree representation of the sentence. Each node in the parse tree represents a vector of dimension **n** corresponding to that word or phrase in the sentence.

3.2 Unfolding Recursive Autoencoders with Dynamic Pooling

Socher et al.(2011) first used Unfolding Recursive Autoencoders with dynamic pooling for the purpose of paraphrase identification. We would be using their method in our paper for sentence alignment. We learn the embeddings of all the phrases in the parse tree of the sentences using unfolding RAE. For a given sentence with **N** words, we have total $2\mathbf{N} - 1$ nodes in the parse tree of the sentence, **N** for the words and $\mathbf{N} - 1$ for the internal nodes or phrases in the sentence as determined by the parsing of the sentence.

For computing the similarity matrix for two sentences, the rows and columns denote the words in their original sentence order. We then add to each row and column the nonterminal nodes of the parse tree in a depth-first and right-to-left order.

For a sentence with N words, and with word embeddings $x_{1:N}$ and RAE encoding for phrases $y_{1:N-1}$, form

$$s = [x_1, ..., x_N, y_1, ..., y_{N-1}] \qquad (5)$$

For two sentences (s_1, s_2), the similarity matrix S contains the Euclidean distance between $(s_1)_i$ and $(s_2)_j$.

$$(S)_{i,j} = \|(s_1)_i - (s_2)_j\|^2 \qquad (6)$$

For sentence s_1 of size n and sentence s_2 of size m, the matrix has dimension $(2n-1) \times (2m-1)$. Since the resulting similarity matrix has dimension which depends on the lengths of the given sentences, we would use dynamic pooling to convert it into a matrix of fixed dimension.

We would be using dynamic min-pooling to convert the variable sized matrix into a matrix of size $n_p \times n_p$. As Socher et al.(2011) reported, the best suited size for n_p is 15. For dynamic pooling, we divide each dimension of 2D matrix into n_p chunks of $\left\lfloor \frac{len}{n_p} \right\rfloor$ size, where len is the length of dimension. If the length len of any dimension is lesser than n_p, we duplicate the matrix entries along that dimension till len becomes greater than or equal to n_p. If there are l leftover entries where $l = len - n_p * \left\lfloor \frac{len}{n_p} \right\rfloor$, we distribute them to the last l chunks. We do it for both the dimensions.

We are using min-pooling because closer the two phrases are, lesser is the euclidean distance between them. Min-pooling would be able to capture this relationship if there are two phrases in the window which are closer to each other.

3.3 Alignment using similarity scores

The fixed dimension matrix obtained in the previous step was fed to the softmax classifier to get a confidence score about similarity between sentences. We would use a dynamic programming algorithm to find the optimum alignment of sentences between the documents. This approach relies on the document comparability and linearity of sentence ordering in the two documents (albeit weak). We find the maximum optimum alignment between two documents and then backtrack using the alignment matrix M to find the sentences that were aligned. Here, $M(i,j)$ denotes the maximum alignment between sentences $1..i$ of one document to sentences $1..j$ of the other document and $sim(i,j)$ denotes the confidence score as given by softmax classifier for similarity between sentences i and j of the two documents respectively. The $offdiag$ constant is used to skip a match between two sentences if the similarity between them is very low. The value of $offdiag$ constant was cho-

sen to be 0.1 for our experiment.

$$M(i,j) = \max \begin{cases} M(i-1,j-1) + sim(i,j) \\ M(i-1,j) + offdiag \\ M(i,j-1) + offdiag \end{cases} \tag{7}$$

4 Experiment

We would list below the detailed steps of our experiment,

4.1 Unfolding RAE's training

We used a pre-trained model of RAE's as given by Socher et al.(2011) which is trained using a subset of 150,000 sentences from the NYT and AP sections of the Gigaword corpus. They used Stanford parser(De Marneffe et al., 2006) to create the parse trees for all sentences. 100-dimensional vectors computed via the unsupervised method of Collobert and Weston (Collobert and Weston, 2008) and provided by Turian et al.(Turian et al., 2010) were used. The RAE used had two encoding layers. The size of hidden layer used is 200 units.

4.2 Softmax Classifier

For training the softmax classifier to get the similarity scores between two sentences, we used the dataset for similar task i.e. Paraphrase Identification for training as both the tasks are similar when only individual sentences irrespective of their context are considered. Microsoft Research paraphrase corpus (MSRPC) consists of 5801 pairs of sentences which have been extracted from news sources on the web, along with human annotations indicating whether each pair captures a paraphrase/semantic equivalence relationship.All sentences are labeled by two annotators who agreed in 83% of the cases and third annotator resolved the conflicts. A total of 3,900 sentence pairs are labeled as paraphrases. We used the standard split of 70-30 for training and testing.

4.3 Dataset

For testing our algorithm we took articles literacynet archives[2]. It maintains a collection of stories from CNN and CBF5. The material is intended to be used for promoting the literacy. Each story in the archive has an abridged or shorter version. We

---

[2]http://literacynet.org

took 5 such pairs of stories and their abridged versions leading two 2033 sentence pairs that could potentially be aligned. We manually annotated the dataset to find the ground truth. The alignment diversity measure (ADM) for two texts, T_1, T_2, is defined to be:

$$ADM(T_1, T_2) = \frac{2 \times matches(T_1, T_2)}{|T_1| + |T_2|} \quad (8)$$

where $matches$ denote the actual number of aligned sentence pairs between two documents. Intuitively, for closely aligned document pairs, as prevalent in bilingual alignment or MT tasks, one would expect an ADM value close to 1. The average ADM in our dataset is 0.61.

4.4 Algorithm

1. Given two texts T_1, T_2, we split each into its sentences. For all sentences s_i in T_1 and for all sentences s'_j in T_2, we generate the embedding vectors for all the words and phrases in the sentences using unfolding RAE.

2. The similarity matrix S is generated for s_i and s'_j by taking Euclidean distance of between all the possible words and phrases of both the sentences as mentioned earlier.

3. Each similarity matrix is converted to fixed size matrix S_{pooled} by using dynamic Min-pooling and is fed to softmax classifier which assigns the confidence score of the two sentences being similar. Now, we have matrix P for all the sentence pairs in T_1 and T_2 such that $P_{i,j}$ represents a measure of similarity between s_i in T_1 and s'_j in T_2.

4. Let $M_{i,j}$ denote the maximum similarity score obtained by aligning the sentences $s_{1:i}$ of T_1 with sentences $s'_{1:j}$ of T_2. We then use a dynamic programming algorithm to maximize this score. We also store the choices made at each step of dynamic programming algorithm and back track to find the optimum sentence alignment.

5. Additionally, we can use heuristics like allowing mapping of multiple sentences in the vicinity of the given sentence to the corresponding sentence in other document, such as to cover cases of splitting a sentence into sentences or vice-versa. But such cases occur rarely and this step can safely be neglected.

4.5 Results

To evaluate our result, we also implemented the Nelken and Shieber(2006)'s approach to compare their results with our results and get a better idea of our method's performance. We chose Nelken's(2006) approach because they have shown that it out performs all other methods. We tested our algorithm on the dataset and found that our approach yielded a precision of 78.84% on a recall of 67.21% giving us an F1-score of 0.7256 . While on the same dataset, Nelken and Shieber's approach gave 65.95% precision on a recall of 50.81% and thus an F1-score of 0.5739. Thus, our approach clearly outperforms Neilken and Shieber's approach. It is to be noted that Nelken and Shieber report an F1-score of 0.6676 at a recall of 0.558, while our implementation of their approach achieved an F1-score of 0.5739 at recall of 0.508. The change in F1-score may be because of the different types of dataset used in the two experiments. Nelken and Shieber had used Britannica encyclopedia and its elementary version containing information about the cities. We have used news reports and their abridged versions which used widely divergent language forms, such as abundant use of change of tense, change of grammatical person, change of writing style etc. which could not be captured by their TF-IDF based similarity. Fig. 1 shows one instance of alignment of a document pair by our approach vs. the gold alignment.

Approach	Precision	Recall	F1-score
RAE+Pool+Align	0.7884	0.6721	0.7256
Nelken's	0.6595	0.5081	0.5739

Table 1: Results of different approaches on dataset

5 Conclusion

We have presented a novel algorithm for aligning the sentences of monolingual corpora of comparable documents. We used a neural network model to arrive at a measure of similarity between sentences. The contextual information present in the document was leveraged upon by using a dynamic programming algorithm to align sentences. Our algorithm performed better than the baseline implementation. It takes into account the semantics being conveyed by the sentences rather just relying on the bag-of-words model for sentence similarity

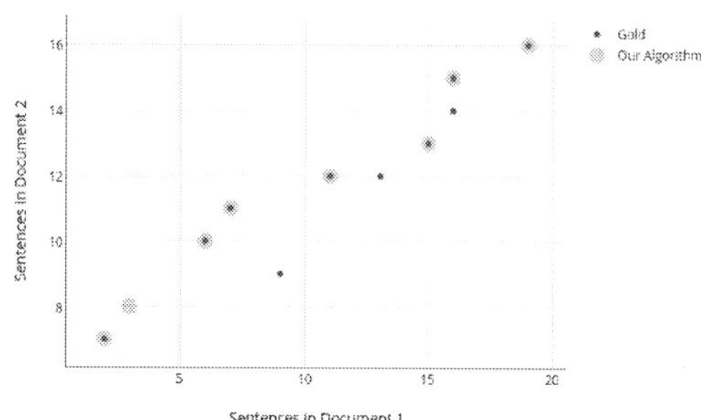

Figure 1: Gold Assignment vs Our Approach on an example. The orange circles with blue dot denote True Positives, orange circles denote False Positives and the blue dots denote False Negatives.

function.

Acknowledgments

We would like to thank all the anonymous reviewers for their valuable feedback.

References

Regina Barzilay and Noemie Elhadad. 2003. Sentence alignment for monolingual comparable corpora. In *Proceedings of the 2003 conference on Empirical methods in natural language processing*. Association for Computational Linguistics, pages 25–32.

Yoshua Bengio, Réjean Ducharme, Pascal Vincent, and Christian Jauvin. 2003. A neural probabilistic language model. *journal of machine learning research* 3(Feb):1137–1155.

Paul Clough, Robert Gaizauskas, Scott SL Piao, and Yorick Wilks. 2002. Meter: Measuring text reuse. In *Proceedings of the 40th Annual Meeting on Association for Computational Linguistics*. Association for Computational Linguistics, pages 152–159.

Ronan Collobert and Jason Weston. 2008. A unified architecture for natural language processing: Deep neural networks with multitask learning. In *Proceedings of the 25th international conference on Machine learning*. ACM, pages 160–167.

Marie-Catherine De Marneffe, Bill MacCartney, Christopher D Manning, et al. 2006. Generating typed dependency parses from phrase structure parses. In *Proceedings of LREC*. volume 6, pages 449–454.

Bill Dolan, Chris Quirk, and Chris Brockett. 2004. Unsupervised construction of large paraphrase corpora: Exploiting massively parallel news sources. In *Proceedings of the 20th international conference on Computational Linguistics*. Association for Computational Linguistics, page 350.

Vasileios Hatzivassiloglou, Judith L Klavans, Melissa L Holcombe, Regina Barzilay, Min-Yen Kan, and Kathleen R McKeown. 2001. Simfinder: A flexible clustering tool for summarization. In *Proceedings of the NAACL workshop on automatic summarization*. volume 1.

Erwin Marsi and Emiel Krahmer. 2005. Explorations in sentence fusion. In *Proceedings of the European Workshop on Natural Language Generation*. Citeseer, pages 109–117.

Tomas Mikolov, Wen-tau Yih, and Geoffrey Zweig. 2013. Linguistic regularities in continuous space word representations. In *HLT-NAACL*. volume 13, pages 746–751.

Saul B Needleman and Christian D Wunsch. 1970. A general method applicable to the search for similarities in the amino acid sequence of two proteins. *Journal of molecular biology* 48(3):443–453.

Rani Nelken and Stuart M Shieber. 2006. Towards robust context-sensitive sentence alignment for monolingual corpora. In *EACL*.

Jeffrey Pennington, Richard Socher, and Christopher D Manning. 2014. Glove: Global vectors for word representation. In *EMNLP*. volume 14, pages 1532–1543.

Richard Socher, Eric H. Huang, Jeffrey Pennington, Andrew Y. Ng, and Christopher D. Manning. 2011. Dynamic Pooling and Unfolding Recursive Autoencoders for Paraphrase Detection. In *Advances in Neural Information Processing Systems 24*.

Joseph Turian, Lev Ratinov, and Yoshua Bengio. 2010. Word representations: a simple and general method for semi-supervised learning. In *Proceedings of the 48th annual meeting of the association for computational linguistics*. Association for Computational Linguistics, pages 384–394.

Acquisition of Translation Lexicons for Historically Unwritten Languages via Bridging Loanwords

Michael Bloodgood
Department of Computer Science
The College of New Jersey
Ewing, NJ 08628
mbloodgood@tcnj.edu

Benjamin Strauss
Computer Science and Engineering Dept.
The Ohio State University
Columbus, OH 43210
strauss.105@osu.edu

Abstract

With the advent of informal electronic communications such as social media, colloquial languages that were historically unwritten are being written for the first time in heavily code-switched environments. We present a method for inducing portions of translation lexicons through the use of expert knowledge in these settings where there are approximately zero resources available other than a language informant, potentially not even large amounts of monolingual data. We investigate inducing a Moroccan Darija-English translation lexicon via French loanwords bridging into English and find that a useful lexicon is induced for human-assisted translation and statistical machine translation.

1 Introduction

With the explosive growth of informal electronic communications such as email, social media, web comments, etc., colloquial languages that were historically unwritten are starting to be written for the first time. For these languages, there are extremely limited (approximately zero) resources available, not even large amounts of monolingual text data or possibly not even small amounts of monolingual text data. Even when audio resources are available, difficulties arise when converting sound to text (Tratz et al., 2013; Robinson and Gadelii, 2003). Moreover, the text data that can be obtained often has non-standard spellings and substantial code-switching with other traditionally written languages (Tratz et al., 2013).

In this paper we present a method for the acquisition of translation lexicons via loanwords and expert knowledge that requires zero resources of the borrowing language. Many historically unwritten languages borrow from highly resourced languages. Also, it is often feasible to locate a language expert to find out how sounds in these languages would be rendered if they were to be written as many of them are beginning to be written in social media, etc. We thus expect the general method to be applicable for multiple historically unwritten languages. In this paper we investigate inducing a Moroccan Darija-English translation lexicon via borrowed French words. Moroccan Darija is an historically unwritten dialect of Arabic spoken by millions but lacking in standardization and linguistic resources (Tratz et al., 2013). Moroccan Darija is known to borrow many words from French, one of the most highly resourced languages in the world. By mapping Moroccan Darija-French borrowings to their donor French words, we can rapidly create lexical resources for portions of Moroccan Darija vocabulary for which no resources currently exist. For example, we could use one of many bilingual French-English dictionaries to bridge into English and create a Moroccan Darija-English translation lexicon that can be used to assist professional translation of Moroccan Darija into English and to assist with construction of Moroccan Darija-English Machine Translation (MT) systems.

The rest of this paper is structured as follows. Section 2 summarizes related work; section 3 explains our method; section 4 discusses experimental results of applying our method to the case of building a Moroccan Darija-English translation lexicon; and section 5 concludes.

2 Related Work

Translation lexicons are a core resource used for multilingual processing of languages. Manual creation of translation lexicons by lexicographers is

Proceedings of the 10th Workshop on Building and Using Comparable Corpora, pages 21–25,
Vancouver, Canada, August 3, 2017. ©2017 Association for Computational Linguistics

time-consuming and expensive. There are more than 7000 languages in the world, many of which are historically unwritten (Lewis et al., 2015). For a relatively small number of these languages there are extensive resources available that have been manually created. It has been noted by others (Mann and Yarowsky, 2001; Schafer and Yarowsky, 2002) that languages are organized into families and that using cognates between sister languages can help rapidly create translation lexicons for lower-resourced languages. For example, the methods in (Mann and Yarowsky, 2001) are able to detect that English *kilograms* maps to Portuguese *quilogramas* via bridge Spanish *kilogramos*. This general idea has been worked on extensively in the context of cognates detection, with 'cognate' typically re-defined to include loanwords as well as true cognates. The methods use monolingual data at a minimum and many signals such as orthographic similarity, phonetic similarity, contextual similarity, temporal similarity, frequency similarity, burstiness similarity, and topic similarity (Bloodgood and Strauss, 2017; Irvine and Callison-Burch, 2013; Kondrak et al., 2003; Schafer and Yarowsky, 2002; Mann and Yarowsky, 2001). Inducing translations via loanwords was specifically targeted in (Tsvetkov and Dyer, 2015; Tsvetkov et al., 2015). While some of these methods don't require bilingual resources, with the possible exception of small bilingual seed dictionaries, they do at a minimum require monolingual text data in the languages to be modeled and sometimes have specific requirements on the monolingual text data such as having text coming from the same time period for each of the languages being modeled. For colloquial languages that were historically unwritten, but that are now starting to be written with the advent of social media and web comments, there are often extremely limited resources of any type available, not even large amounts of monolingual text data. Moreover, the written data that can be obtained often has non-standard spellings and code-switching with other traditionally written languages. Often the code-switching occurs within words whereby the base is borrowed and the affixes are not borrowed, analogous to the multi-language categories "V" and "N" from (Mericli and Bloodgood, 2012). The data available for historically unwritten languages, and especially the lack thereof, is not suitable for previously developed cognates detection

methods that operate as discussed above. In the next section we present a method for translation lexicon induction via loanwords that uses expert knowledge and requires zero resources from the borrowing language other than a language informant.

3 Method

Our method is to take word pronunciations from the donor language we are using and convert them to how they would be rendered in the borrowing language if they were to be borrowed. These are our candidate loanwords. There are three possible cases for a given generated candidate loanword string:

true match string occurs in borrowing language and is a loanword from the donor language;

false match string occurs in borrowing language by coincidence but it's not a loanword from the donor language;

no match string does not occur in borrowing language.

For the case of inducing a Moroccan Darija-English translation lexicon via French we start with a French-English bilingual dictionary and take all the French pronunciations in IPA (International Phonetic Alphabet)[1] and convert them to how they would be rendered in Arabic script. For this we created a multiple-step transliteration process:

Step 1 Break pronunciation into syllables.

Step 2 Convert each IPA syllable to a string in modified Buckwalter transliteration[2], which supports a one-to-one mapping to Arabic script.

Step 3 Convert each syllable's string in modified Buckwalter transliteration to Arabic script.

Step 4 Merge the resulting Arabic script strings for each syllable to generate a candidate loanword string.

---

[1] `https://en.wikipedia.org/wiki/International_Phonetic_Alphabet`

[2] The modified version of Buckwalter transliteration, `https://en.wikipedia.org/wiki/Buckwalter_transliteration`, replaces special characters such as < and > with alphanumeric characters so that the transliterations are safe for use with other standards such as XML (Extensible Markup Language). For more information see (Habash, 2010).

For syllabification, for many word pronunciations the syllables are already marked in the IPA by the '.' character; if syllables are not already marked in the IPA, we run a simple syllabifier to complete step 1. For step 2, we asked a language expert to give us a sequence of rules to convert a syllable's pronunciation to modified Buckwalter transliteration. This is itself a multi-step process (see next paragraph for details). In step 3, we simply do the one-to-one conversion and obtain Arabic script for each syllable. In step 4, we merge the Arabic script for each syllable and get the generated candidate loanword string.

The multi-step process that takes place in step 2 of the process is:

Step 2.1 Make minor vowel adjustments in certain contexts, e.g., when 'a' is between two consonants it is changed to 'A'.

Step 2.2 Perform bulk of conversion by using table of mappings from IPA characters to modified Buckwalter characters such as 'a'→'a', 'k'→'k', 'y:'→'iy', etc. that were supplied by a language expert.

Step 2.3 Perform miscellaneous modifications to finalize the modified Buckwalter strings, e.g., if a syllable ends in 'a', then append an 'A' to that syllable.

The entire conversion process is illustrated in Figure 1 for the French word *raconteur*. At the top of the Figure is the IPA from the French dictionary entry with syllables marked. At the next level, step 1 (syllabification) has been completed. Step 2.1 doesn't apply to any of the syllables in this word since there are no minor vowel adjustments that are applicable for this word so at the next level each syllable is shown after step 2.2 has been completed. The next level shows the syllables after step 2.3 has been completed. The next level shows after step 3 has been completed and then at the end the strings are merged to form the candidate loanword.

4   Experiments and Discussion

In our experiments we extracted a French-English bilingual dictionary using the freely available English Wiktionary dump 20131101 downloaded from `http://dumps.wikimedia.org/enwiktionary`. From this dump we extracted all the French words, their pronunciations,

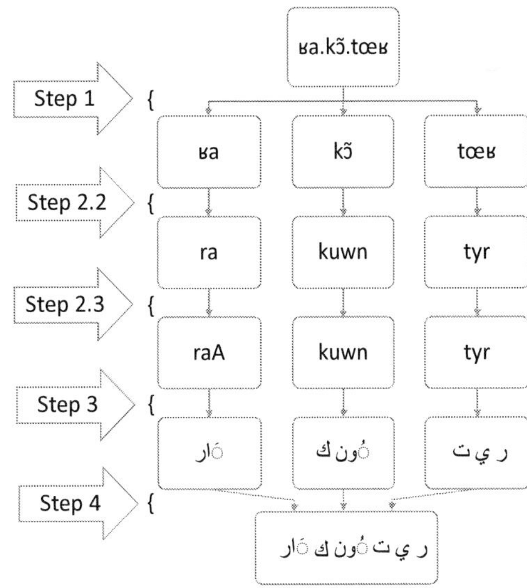

Figure 1: Example of French to Arabic Process for the French word *raconteur*. As discussed in the main text, step 2.1 doesn't apply to this example so it is omitted from the diagram to conserve space. Note that in the final step the word is in order of Unicode codepoints. Then application software that is capable of processing Arabic will render that as a proper Arabic string in right-to-left order with proper character joining adjustments as راكونتير

and their English definitions. Using the process described in section 3 to convert each of the French pronunciations into Arabic script yielded 8277 unique loanword candidate strings.

The data used for testing consists of a million lines of user comments crawled from the Moroccan news website `http://www.hespress.com`. The crawled user comments contain Moroccan Darija in heavily code-switched environments. While this makes for a challenging setting, it is a realistic representation of the types of environments in which historically unwritten languages are being written for the first time. The data we used is consistent with well-known code-switching among Arabic speakers, extending spoken discourse into formal writing (Bentahila and Davies, 1983; Redouane, 2005). The total number of tokens in our Hespress corpus is 18,781,041. We found that 1150 of our 8277 loanword candidates appear in our Hespress corpus. Moreover, more than a million (1169087) loanword candi-

Annotator	Arabic	Unknown	French	Total
A	907	88	190	1185
B	812	174	199	1185

Table 1: Number of word instances annotated.

date instances appear in the corpus. Recall that a match could be a true match that really is a French loanword or a false match that just happens to coincidentally have string equality with words in the borrowing language, but is not a French loanword. False matches are particularly likely to occur for very short words. Accordingly, we filter out candidates that are of length less than four characters. This leaves us with 838 candidates appearing in the corpus and 217616 candidate instances in the corpus. To get an idea of what percentage of our matches are true matches versus false matches, we conducted an annotation exercise with two native Moroccan Darija speakers who also knew at least intermediate French. We pulled a random sample[3] of 1185 candidate instances from our corpus and asked each annotator to mark each instance as either:

A if the instance is originally from Arabic,

F if the instance is originally from French, or

U if they were not sure.

The results are shown in Table 1. There are a substantial number of French loanwords that are found. Some examples of translations successfully induced by our method are:

omelette أومليت; and

bourgeoisie بورجوازي.

We hypothesize that our method can help improve machine translation (MT) of historically unwritten dialects with nearly zero resources. To test this hypothesis, we ran an MT experiment as follows.

First we selected a random set of sentences from the Hespress corpus that each contained at least one candidate instance and had an MSA/Moroccan Darija/English trilingual translator translate them into English. In total, 273 sentences were translated. This served as our test set.

We trained a baseline MT system using all GALE MSA-English parallel corpora available from the Linguistic Data Consortium (LDC) from 2007 to 2013.[4]

We trained the system using Moses 3.0 with default parameters. This baseline system achieves BLEU score of 7.48 on our difficult test set of code-switched Moroccan Darija and MSA.

We trained a second system using the parallel corpora with our induced Moroccan Darija-English translation lexicon appended to the end of the training data. This time the BLEU score increased to 8.11, a gain of .63 BLEU points.

5 Conclusions

With the explosive growth of informal textual electronic communications such as social media, web comments, etc., many colloquial everyday languages that were historically unwritten are now being written for the first time often in heavily code-switched text with traditionally written languages. The new written versions of these languages pose significant challenges for multilingual processing technology due to Out-Of-Vocabulary (OOV) challenges. Yet it is relatively common that these historically unwritten languages borrow significant amounts of vocabulary from relatively well resourced written languages. We presented a method for translation lexicon induction via loanwords for alleviating the OOV challenges in these settings where the borrowing language has extremely limited amounts of resources available, in many cases not even substantial amounts of monolingual data that is typically exploited by previous cognates and loanword detection methods to induce translation lexicons. This paper demonstrates induction of a Moroccan Darija-English translation lexicon via bridging French loanwords using the method and in MT experiments, the addition of the induced Moroccan Darija-English lexicon increased system performance by .63 BLEU points.

Acknowledgments

We would like to thank Tim Buckwalter for his support and for providing us with the initial mapping of IPA syllables to their corresponding Arabic orthographies as well as the contextual adjustment rules that we used in our experiments.

---

[3]We removed 15 Arabic stopwords from our candidate list before pulling the random sample.

[4]The LDC catalog numbers for the corpora we used are: LDC2008T09, LDC2007T24, LDC2008T02, LDC2009T09, LDC2009T03, LDC2012T14, LDC2012T06, LDC2012T17, LDC2012T18, LDC2013T01, and LDC2013T14.

References

Abdelali Bentahila and Eirlys E Davies. 1983. The syntax of Arabic-French code-switching. *Lingua* 59(4):301–330.

Michael Bloodgood and Benjamin Strauss. 2017. Using global constraints and reranking to improve cognates detection. In *Proceedings of the 55th Annual Meeting of the Association for Computational Linguistics*. Association for Computational Linguistics, Vancouver, Canada. https://arxiv.org/abs/1704.07050.

Nizar Habash. 2010. *Introduction to Arabic Natural Language Processing*. Synthesis lectures on human language technologies. Morgan & Claypool Publishers. https://books.google.com/books?id=kRIHCnC74BoC.

Ann Irvine and Chris Callison-Burch. 2013. Supervised bilingual lexicon induction with multiple monolingual signals. In *Proceedings of the 2013 Conference of the North American Chapter of the Association for Computational Linguistics: Human Language Technologies*. Association for Computational Linguistics, Atlanta, Georgia, pages 518–523. http://www.aclweb.org/anthology/N13-1056.

Grzegorz Kondrak, Daniel Marcu, and Kevin Knight. 2003. Cognates can improve statistical translation models. In *Proceedings of the 2003 Conference of the North American Chapter of the Association for Computational Linguistics on Human Language Technology: Companion Volume of the Proceedings of HLT-NAACL 2003–short Papers - Volume 2*. Association for Computational Linguistics, Stroudsburg, PA, USA, NAACL-Short '03, pages 46–48. http://www.aclweb.org/anthology/N/N03/N03-2016.pdf.

M. Paul Lewis, Gary F. Simons, and Charles D. Fennig. 2015. *Ethnologue: Languages of the world*, volume 18. SIL international, Dallas, TX.

Gideon S. Mann and David Yarowsky. 2001. Multipath translation lexicon induction via bridge languages. In *Proceedings of the second meeting of the North American Chapter of the Association for Computational Linguistics on Language technologies*. Association for Computational Linguistics, Stroudsburg, PA, USA, NAACL '01, pages 1–8. http://www.aclweb.org/anthology/N/N01/N01-1020.pdf.

Benjamin S. Mericli and Michael Bloodgood. 2012. Annotating cognates and etymological origin in Turkic languages. In *Proceedings of the First Workshop on Language Resources and Technologies for Turkic Languages*. European Language Resources Association, Istanbul, Turkey, pages 47–51. http://arxiv.org/abs/1501.03191.

Rabia Redouane. 2005. Linguistic constraints on codeswitching and codemixing of bilingual Moroccan Arabic-French speakers in Canada. In *ISB4: Proceedings of the 4th International Symposium on Bilingualism*. pages 1921–1933.

Clinton Robinson and Karl Gadelii. 2003. Writing unwritten languages, a guide to the process. *Paris: UNESCO. Retrieved June 24, 2008* .

Charles Schafer and David Yarowsky. 2002. Inducing translation lexicons via diverse similarity measures and bridge languages. In *Proceedings of the 6th Conference on Natural language Learning - Volume 20*. Association for Computational Linguistics, Stroudsburg, PA, USA, pages 1–7. http://www.aclweb.org/anthology/W/W02/W02-2026.pdf.

Stephen Tratz, Douglas Briesch, Jamal Laoudi, and Clare Voss. 2013. Tweet conversation annotation tool with a focus on an arabic dialect, moroccan darija. In *Proceedings of the 7th Linguistic Annotation Workshop and Interoperability with Discourse*. Association for Computational Linguistics, Sofia, Bulgaria, pages 135–139. http://www.aclweb.org/anthology/W13-2317.

Yulia Tsvetkov, Waleed Ammar, and Chris Dyer. 2015. Constraint-based models of lexical borrowing. In *Proceedings of the 2015 Conference of the North American Chapter of the Association for Computational Linguistics: Human Language Technologies*. Association for Computational Linguistics, Denver, Colorado, pages 598–608. http://www.aclweb.org/anthology/N15-1062.

Yulia Tsvetkov and Chris Dyer. 2015. Lexicon stratification for translating out-of-vocabulary words. In *Proceedings of the 53rd Annual Meeting of the Association for Computational Linguistics and the 7th International Joint Conference on Natural Language Processing (Volume 2: Short Papers)*. Association for Computational Linguistics, Beijing, China, pages 125–131. http://www.aclweb.org/anthology/P15-2021.

Toward a Comparable Corpus of Latvian, Russian and English Tweets

Dmitrijs Milajevs
NIST
Gaithersburg, MD, USA
dmitrijs.milajevs@nist.gov

Abstract

Twitter has become a rich source for linguistic data. Here, a possibility of building a trilingual Latvian-Russian-English corpus of tweets from Riga, Latvia is investigated. Such a corpus, once constructed, might be of great use for multiple purposes including training machine translation models, examining cross-lingual phenomena and studying the population of Riga. This pilot study shows that it is feasible to build such a resource by collecting and analysing a pilot corpus, which is made publicly available and can be used to construct a large comparable corpus.

1 Introduction

Comparable corpora are widely used by the natural language processing community to build machine translation or information retrieval models. The goal of this work is to investigate in a pilot study whether it is possible to build a comparable linguistic resource of tweets that originates from one specific location–Riga, Latvia. Riga is a great location for this because it is a multilingual city in which Latvian and Russian are both widely used in everyday life, and English is a lingua franca in tourism and commerce.

Despite the fact that Latvian and Russian are widely used, there is little interaction between the two ethnic communities. The local media consists of two subsystems (Latvian and Russian) which use different sources and present different views on current affairs (Muižnieks, 2010). Even though large media portals tend to have separate Latvian and Russian web-sites, the same opinions are found in comments to controversial content on both versions of web-sites, making the Internet a public space for a dialogue between the ethnic communities (Šulmane, 2010). A corpus of user generated content from Riga is a fruitful resource for studying the integration of the two communities, by identifying what is being discussed; how, and most importantly why it is being discussed.

The pilot corpus[1] consists of tweets over the period of 5 months (November 2016 to March 2017). The main goal of the analysis is to investigate whether a creation of a comparable tweet corpus is feasible and what the corpus construction strategy should be. To see whether the pilot corpus is comparable, the peaks of Twitter usage were analysed. These peaks correspond to real world events (national celebrations, international political affairs and weather). The events are actively discussed in all languages, but in different proportions (Section 4).

All three languages are represented: 45.5% tweets are in Latvian, 33.9% in Russian and 20.7% in English.[2] By studying users' tweeting habits, we see that the majority of users (83.3%) mostly tweets in one language (Section 5), making the tweet collection strategy that considers only multilingual users incomplete.

The properties of the corpus correspond to the expectation that it will reflect the real world events and language use proportion, but its size is too small to draw solid conclusions. However, the construction of a reliable comparable corpus is a matter of the data collection procedure and corpus' application, because, as this study shows, not all topics are discussed equally.

2 Related work

Twitter provides an easy way to build a large text corpus for research. Numerous tweet collections are built for a variety of purposes. For example,

---

[1] https://doi.org/10.5281/zenodo.582300
[2] The ratio of ethnic Latvians to Russians in Riga is 46.2% to 37.7%.

Proceedings of the 10th Workshop on Building and Using Comparable Corpora, pages 26–30,
Vancouver, Canada, August 3, 2017. ©2017 Association for Computational Linguistics

Tjong Kim Sang and van den Bosch (2013) discuss the process of building a large collection of Dutch tweets and challenges of accessing the data. Their retrieval method is based on a list of frequent Dutch words.

Vicente et al. (2016) build a parallel multilingual corpus of tweets. Their process consists of two parts: retrieval and alignment. Retrieval is based on a list of multilingual users. The collected tweets are aligned using crowdsourcing. Ling et al. (2013) automatically extract parallel segments from Sina Weibo (a Chinese counterpart of Twitter). Gotti et al. (2013) use the parallel web pages mentioned in tweets of the agencies and organisations of Canada to train a statistical machine translation model.

There is a small but growing body of research of the Latvian Twittersphere, for example, work on sentiment analysis (Peisenieks and Skadiņš, 2014) and opinion mining (Špats and Birzniece, 2016). Both studies focus on Latvian.

3   Dataset construction

The initial set of tweets was retrieved by subscribing to the `POST status/filter` endpoint of the Twitter Streaming API.[3] The collected tweets had to be geo-located and had to originate from the area of Riga, the capital of Latvia.[4]

251 083 tweets were collected within the period from the 1st of November 2016 to the 31st of March 2017. On April 14th 2017, the collection was rehydrated[5] by querying the Twitter API with the collected tweet IDs to get rid of the deleted tweets. In addition, the tweets that originated from retweets were added to the collection: the JSON[6] representation of a retweet includes the original tweet, which was extracted and added to the collection. The rehydrated and expanded collection resulted in a total of 220 883 tweets.

Further analysis of the extended rehydrated collection showed that there are 23 115 (10.5%) tweets that originated from check-ins on Foursquare.[7] This motivated additional filtering of the rehydrated collection, as "check-in

---

[3]`https://dev.twitter.com/streaming/reference/post/statuses/filter`

[4]The `locations` parameter was set to `23.9325829, 56.8570671, 24.3247299, 57.0859184`

[5]Since distribution of raw tweet data is not allowed, tweets IDs are shared instead. Hydration is the process of retrieval of raw tweet data by IDs.

[6]`http://json.org`

[7]`https://foursquare.com`

tweets" follow a predefined template most of the time and thus do not reflect real language use.

Client	Tweet count	Share %
Twitter Web Client	93 705	42.4%
Twitter for iPhone	47 721	21.6%
Twitter for Android	34 277	15.5%
Foursquare*	23 115	10.5%
Instagram*	13 196	5.0%
Twitter for iPad	2 420	1.1%
Endomondo*	1 611	0.7%
Tweetbot of iOS	1 411	0.6%
World Cities*	1 361	0.6%
Linkis*	660	0.3%

Table 1: The top ten of Twitter clients in the rehydrated collection. *Clients that are not included in the final collection as they do not exhibit linguistic value.

Table 1 shows the top ten most popular clients in the rehydrated collection. Together with the tweets originating from Foursquare, tweets from Instagram, an image sharing service, and Endomondo, a workout tracking service, were removed. Tweets written using the World Cities client, which posts weather reports, and the Linkis client—a promotion website—were also removed.

The final collection resulted in 136 067 tweets which are in Latvian, Russian or English and created after the 1st of November 2016. The language of a tweet is provided by the corresponding field in the tweet JSON representation.

4   Tweet analysis

Out of 136 067 tweets that constitute the final collection, 45.5% are in Latvian, 33.9% are in Russian and 20.7% are in English, see Table 2 for tweet counts.

Language	Tweet count	Share %	Avg. token count
Latvian	61 869	45.4%	15
Russian	46 070	33.9%	11
English	28 128	20.7%	14

Table 2: Language distribution in the final collection.

Figure 1 shows the number of tweets per day over time for all three languages. There are several peaks in Twitter usage. Some of them affect all three languages, as in early January, some of them affect only one language, as in late January.

If the Twitter behaviour is affected by events in the real world, then these peaks should correspond

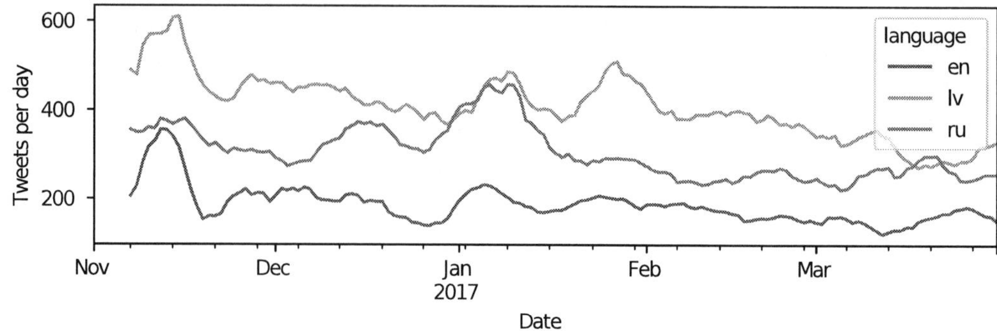

Figure 1: Tweet counts per day per language. The values are averaged over a week window at the right edge.

to events in the real world. The difference in peaks could then be explained as there are different real word events that trigger discussions on Twitter in Latvian, Russian and English. Table 3 suggests, that tweets in Latvian and English share similar behaviour. The Russian tweet timeline is distinct from both timelines, though its behaviour is more similar to the Latvian timeline than to the English.

Language	Latvian	Russian	English
Latvian	1.0	0.4	0.6
Russian	0.4	1.0	0.3
English	0.6	0.3	1.0

Table 3: Pairwise Pearson's-ρ correlation coefficients between Latvian, Russian and English timelines.

What are the distinctive and similar properties of the timelines? To answer the question, we first identify the real world events that happened at the time of the highest peaks.

Mid November   11th of November is Lāčplēsis Day, a memorial day for soldiers who fought for the independence of Latvia. 18 November is the Proclamation Day of the Republic of Latvia. Also, on the 8th of November, the United States presidential election took place.

The number of tweets significantly increased for Latvian and English, and not so much for Russian. Manual inspection of the tweets in that period reveals that the US elections are discussed in all three languages, while the national celebrations of the 11th and the 18th of November are mostly discussed in Latvian. The discussion in-

cludes such topics as the news related to celebrations, historical notes, reminders of working hours of businesses, greeting and advertisement.

Manual inspection also shows that events are language sensitive. For example, the election results were discussed by Latvians in English. Also, businesses reported their working hours during the national celebrations in Latvian and do not duplicate this information in Russian.

Early January   In early January a snowstorm hit Riga. In Latvian and Russian the discussed topics were the same, namely, appreciation of snow, the transportation difficulties and outdoor photos. Tweets in English mostly contained photos showing how beautiful Latvia is in Winter.

Late January   The inauguration of the 45th President of the United States was held on 20th of January 2017. The number of Latvian tweets increases, while for other languages it stays roughly the same. The reason why there are relatively little politics-oriented Russian tweets might be that 60% of citizens and 47% of non-citizens are interested in politics (Aldermane et al., 2000). Out of citizens, 60% are ethnic Latvians, 27% are ethnic Russians. Out of non-citizens, 66% are Russians, and less than 1% are Latvians.[8]

5   User analysis

We have seen an evidence that topics are languge dependant. How many Twitter users switch between languages?

---

[8]`https://lv.wikipedia.org/wiki/Nepilsoņi_(Latvija)`

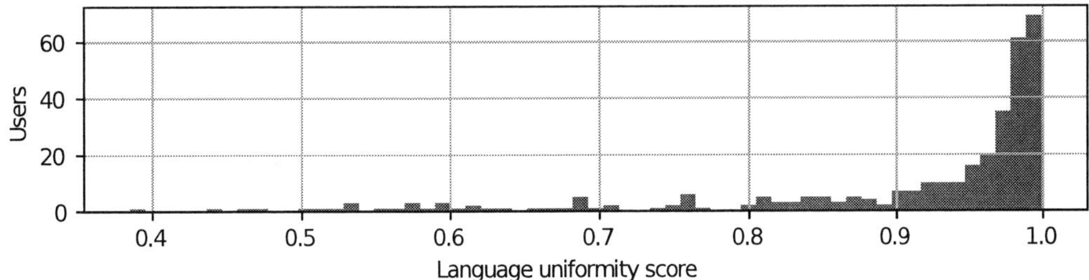

Figure 2: Histogram of language use uniformity scores. Low values mean that distinct languages are used, while high values mean that a single language is preferred.

We consider 507 users for whom at least 50 tweets were collected. 180 or 35.5% of them tweet exclusively in one language (75 users tweet only in Latvian, 43 in Russian and 62 in English). Others tweet in several languages.

To get more insight on how languages are used, we compute the language uniformity score defined as:

$$\frac{\max(n_{lv}, n_{ru}, n_{en})}{n_{lv} + n_{ru} + n_{en}} \quad (1)$$

where n_{lv} corresponds to the number of tweets in Latvian for a given user, n_{ru} to the number of tweets in Russian, and n_{en} to the number of tweets in English.

The higher the score, the more dominant a language. The lowest possible value of 0.33 means that all three languages are used equally. The value of 0.5 means that 50% of tweets are written in a dominant language. The value of 1 means that the user tweets exclusively in one language.

The histogram in Figure 2 shows the score distribution. 420 (82.8%) users tweet mostly in one language (their scores are greater than 0.9). For 83 (16.4%) users the score is between 0.5 and 0.9. There are only four (0.8%) users whose dominant language share is less than 50%.

Among the four Twitter users whose score is less than 0.5—meaning that they use all three languages extensively—three are personal accounts and one is a company account. Other interesting accounts that tweet equally in Latvian and Russian, but do not tweet in English are the accounts of a library and a football club.

To illustrate the language usage pattern between multilingual users, their first most frequently used language, their second most frequently used language and their third most frequently language were identified. If a user tweeted equally in two (three) languages, then the two (three) languages were given the maximal preference. A user who tweeted equally in Latvian and Russian, but less in English, is counted as Latvian and Russian being their first preference, English as the third.

Latvian is not only the most used language among the monoligual users, but also is the first and third most common choice between the multilingual users. The preference for Russian is similar to Latvian, despite the numbers being slightly lower, suggesting its significant role in everyday life. English is almost the ultimate second choice, proving its role as a lingua franca, as Table 4 shows.

	Latvian	Russian	English
Monoligual	**75**	43	62
Multi, first	**150**	135	42
Multi, second	56	19	**266**
Multi, third	**29**	26	9

Table 4: Language preference between users.

6 Conclusion

We have seen that location-based tweet collection produces adequate results. Tweets in all three target languages were collected, and the resulting collection reflects real world events.

How comparable are the language samples within the corpus? Topics are language dependent, so it is not the case that all topics are discussed in every language. There are "monolingual topics" such as the independence day in Latvia. Even "multilingual topics" vary in content, as with the snowstorm tweets, where Latvian and Russian tweets shared common topics, but tweets in English were distinct.

The final answer is that it depends on the application. For machine translation, it is important to have similar content, so the parallel segments can be extracted, for example from Latvian and Russian snowstorm tweets. For a social study, the corpus has to be representative, so that the topics can lead to the analysis of the communities as in the case of why the president inauguration was discussed much less in Russian than in Latvian.

Acknowledgements

The author thanks Dr. Sascha Griffiths for valuable discussion and Tatiana Chepurko for literature suggestions.

Disclaimer

Certain commercial products are identified in this paper in order to specify the experimental procedure adequately. Such identification is not intended to imply recommendation or endorsement by the National Institute of Standards and Technology, nor is it intended to imply that the identified products are necessarily the best available for the purpose.

References

Eiženija Aldermane, Reinis Āboltiņš, Heidi Bottolfs, Boriss Cilēvičs, Jānis Jaudzems, Anita Jākobsone, Ābrams Kleckins, Falks Lange, Jānis Mažeiks, Ilmārs Mežs, Nils Muižnieks, Artis Pabriks, Aija Priedīte, Ilona Stalidzāne, Inese Šūpule, Ramona Umblija, Elmārs Vēbers, and Brigita Zepa. 2000. "Towards a Civic Society-2000" Survey of Latvian Inhabitants. Baltic Institute of Social Sciences.

Fabrizio Gotti, Philippe Langlais, and Atefeh Farzindar. 2013. Translating Government Agencies' Tweet Feeds: Specificities, Problems and (a few) Solutions. In *Proceedings of the Workshop on Language Analysis in Social Media*. Association for Computational Linguistics, Atlanta, Georgia, pages 80–89. http://www.aclweb.org/anthology/W13-1109.

Wang Ling, Guang Xiang, Chris Dyer, Alan Black, and Isabel Trancoso. 2013. Microblogs as Parallel Corpora. In *Proceedings of the 51st Annual Meeting of the Association for Computational Linguistics (Volume 1: Long Papers)*. Association for Computational Linguistics, Sofia, Bulgaria, pages 176–186. http://www.aclweb.org/anthology/P13-1018.

Nils Muižnieks, editor. 2010. *How integrated is Latvian society: An Audit of Achievements, Failures and Challenges*. University of Latvia Press.

Jānis Peisenieks and Raivis Skadiņš. 2014. Uses of Machine Translation in the Sentiment Analysis of Tweets. *Frontiers in Artificial Intelligence and Applications* 268(Human Language Technologies-The Baltic Perspective):126131. https://doi.org/10.3233/978-1-61499-442-8-126.

Gatis Špats and Ilze Birzniece. 2016. Opinion Mining in Latvian Text Using Semantic Polarity Analysis and Machine Learning Approach. *Complex Systems Informatics and Modeling Quarterly* (7):51–59.

Ilze Šulmane. 2010. The Media and Integration. In Nils Muižnieks, editor, *How integrated is Latvian society: An Audit of Achievements, Failures and Challenges*, University of Latvia Press.

Erik Tjong Kim Sang and Antal van den Bosch. 2013. Dealing with big data: The case of Twitter. *Computational Linguistics in the Netherlands Journal* 3:121–134.

Iñaki San Vicente, Iñaki Alegría, Cristina España-Bonet, Pablo Gamallo, Hugo Gonçalo Oliveira, Eva Martínez Garcia, Antonio Toral, Arkaitz Zubiaga, and Nora Aranberri. 2016. TweetMT: A Parallel Microblog Corpus. In Nicoletta Calzolari (Conference Chair), Khalid Choukri, Thierry Declerck, Sara Goggi, Marko Grobelnik, Bente Maegaard, Joseph Mariani, Helene Mazo, Asuncion Moreno, Jan Odijk, and Stelios Piperidis, editors, *Proceedings of the Tenth International Conference on Language Resources and Evaluation (LREC 2016)*. European Language Resources Association (ELRA), Paris, France.

Automatic Extraction of Parallel Speech Corpora
from Dubbed Movies

Alp Öktem[1] and **Mireia Farrús**[1] and **Leo Wanner**[2,1]
[1]Universitat Pompeu Fabra, Spain
[2]Catalan Institute for Research and Advanced Studies (ICREA), Spain

Abstract

This paper presents a methodology to extract parallel speech corpora based on any language pair from dubbed movies, together with an application framework in which some corresponding prosodic parameters are extracted. The obtained parallel corpora are especially suitable for speech-to-speech translation applications when a prosody transfer between source and target languages is desired.

1 Introduction

The availability of large parallel corpora is one of the major challenges in developing translation systems. Bilingual corpora, which are needed to train statistical translation models, are harder to acquire than monolingual corpora since they presuppose the implication of labour in translation or interpretation. Working in the speech domain introduces even more difficulties since interpretations are not sufficient to capture the paralinguistic aspects of speech. Several attempts have been recently made to acquire spoken parallel corpora of considerable size. However, these corpora either do not reflect the prosodic aspects in the interpreted speech or do not carry the traits of natural speech. Or they simply do not align well the source and the target language sides.

To account for this deficit, we propose to exploit dubbed movies where expressive speech is readily available in multiple languages and their corresponding aligned scripts are easily accessible through subtitles. Movies and TV shows have been a good resource for collecting parallel bilingual data because of the availability and open access of subtitles in different languages. With 1850 bitexts of 65 languages, the OpenSubtitles project (Lison and Tiedemann, 2016) is the largest resource of translated movie subtitles compiled so far. The time information in subtitles makes it easy to align sentences of different languages since timing is correlated to the same audio (Itamar and Itai, 2008). In the presence of multiple aligned audio for the same movie, the alignment can be extended to obtain parallel speech corpora. Popular movies, TV shows and documentaries are released with dubbed audio in many countries. Dubbing requires the voice acting of the original speech in another language. Because of this, the dubbed speech carries more or less the same paralinguistic aspects of the original speech.

In what follows, we describe our methodology for the extraction of a speech parallel corpus based on any language pair from dubbed movies. Unlike Tsiartas et al. (2011), who propose a method based on machine learning for automatically extracting bilingual audio-subtitle pairs from movies, we only need raw movie data, and do not require any training. Moreover, our methodology ensures the fulfilment of the following requirements: (a) it is easily expandable, (b) it supports multiple pairs of languages, (c) it can handle any domain and speech style, and (d) it delivers a parallel spoken language corpus with annotated expressive speech. "Expressive speech" annotation means that the corpus is prosodically rich, which is essential to be able to deal with non-neutral speech emotions, as done in increasingly popular speech-to-speech translation applications that try to cope with prosody transfer between source and target utterances (Agüero et al., 2006; Sridhar et al., 2008; Anumanchipalli et al., 2012).

The remainder of the paper is structured as follows. Section 2 reviews the main multilingual parallel speech corpora available to the research community. Section 3 presents the methodology used in the current paper, and Section 4 discusses the current state of the obtained parallel corpora so far.

31

Proceedings of the 10th Workshop on Building and Using Comparable Corpora, pages 31–35,
Vancouver, Canada, August 3, 2017. ©2017 Association for Computational Linguistics

In Section 5, finally, some conclusions are drawn and some aspects of our future work in the context of parallel speech corpora are mentioned.

2 Available Parallel Speech Corpora

As already mentioned above, several attempts have been made to compile large spoken parallel corpora. Such corpora of considerable size are, e.g., the EPIC corpus (Bendazzoli and Sandrelli, 2005), the EMIME Bilingual Database (Wester, 2010), and the Microsoft Speech Language Translation (MSLT) corpus (Federmann and Lewis, 2016). All of them have been manually compiled, and all of them show one or several shortcomings. The EPIC corpus, which has been compiled from speeches from the European Parliament and their interpretations, falls short in reflecting the prosodic aspects in the interpreted speech. The EMIME database is a compilation of prompted speeches and does not capture the natural spoken language traits. The MSLT corpus has been collected in bilingual conversation settings, but there is no one-to-one alignment between sentences in different languages. A summary of the available bilingual speech corpora is listed in Table 1.

3 Methodology

Our multimodal parallel corpus creation consists of three main stages: (1) movie sentence segmentation, (2) prosodic parameter extraction, and (3) parallel sentence alignment. The first and second stages can be seen as a monolingual data creation, as they take the audio and subtitle pairs as input in one language, and output speech/text/prosodic parameters at the sentence level. The resulting monolingual data from stages 1 and 2 are fed into stage 3, where corresponding sentences are aligned and reordered to create the corresponding parallel data. A general overview of the system is presented in Figure 1.

Let us discuss each of these stages in turn.

3.1 Segmentation of movie audio into sentences

This stage involves the extraction of audio and complete sentences from the original audio and the corresponding subtitles of the movie. For subtitles, the SubRip text file format[1] (SRT) is accepted. Each subtitle entry contains the following

information: (i) start time, (ii) end time, and (iii) text of the speech spoken at that time in the movie. The subtitle entries do not necessarily correspond to sentences: a subtitle entry may include more than one sentence, and a sentence can spread over many subtitle entries; consider an example portion of a subtitle:

```
80
00:06:46,114 --> 00:06:48,741
Well, I was stationed
up in Casablanca

81
00:06:48,825 --> 00:06:51,535
at an army field hospital
during the war.

82
00:06:51,995 --> 00:06:53,871
- Do you live in Morocco?
- Yes.
```

The sentence segmentation stage starts with a preprocessing step in which elements that do not correspond to speech are removed. These include: Speaker name markers (e.g., JAMES: . . .), text formatting tags, non-verbal information (laughter, horn, etc.) and speech dashes. Audio is initially segmented according to the timestamps in subtitle entries, with extra 0.5 seconds at each end. Then, each audio segment and its respective subtitle text are sent to the speech aligner software (Vocapia Scribe[2]) to detect word boundaries. This pre-segmentation helps to detect the times of the words that end with a sentence-ending punctuation mark ('.', '?', '!', ':', '...'). Average word boundary confidence score of the word alignment is used to determine whether the sentence will be extracted successfully or not. If the confidence score is above a threshold of 0.5, the initial segment is cut from occurrences of sentence-endings. In a second pass, cut segments that do not end with a sentence-ending punctuation mark are merged with the subsequent segments to form full sentences. We used *Libav*[3] library to perform the audio cuts.

3.2 Prosodic parameter extraction

This stage involves prosodic parameter extraction for each sentence segment detected in stage 1. The *ProsodyPro* library (Xu, 2013) (a script developed for the Praat software (Boersma and Weenink, 2001)) is used to extract prosodic features from speech. As input, ProsodyPro takes the audio of

---

[1] https://www.matroska.org/technical/specs/subtitles/srt.html

[2] https://scribe.vocapia.com/

[3] https://libav.org/

Corpus	Languages	Speech style
EPIC	English, Italian, Spanish	spontaneous/interpreted
MSLT	English, French, German	constrained conversations
EMIME	Finnish/English, German/English	prompted
EMIME Mandarin	Mandarin/English	prompted
MDA (Almeman et al., 2013)	Four Arabic dialects	prompted
Farsi-English (Melvin et al., 2004)	Farsi/English	read/semi-spontaneous

Table 1: Some available parallel speech corpora.

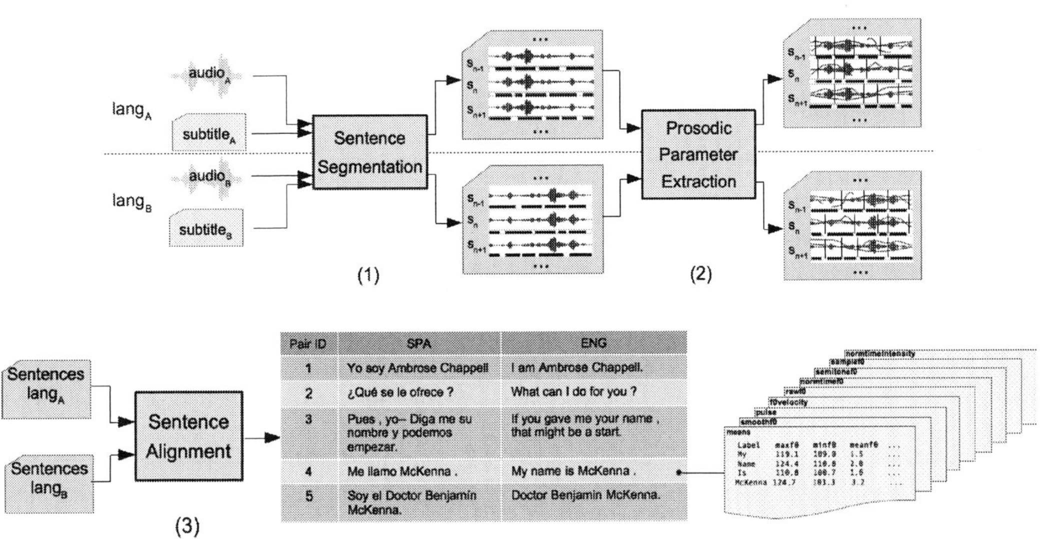

Figure 1: Above: Monolingual corpus creation from different audio-subtitle pairs in parallel. Below: Bilingual parallel corpus creation of the example dataset.

an utterance and a TextGrid file containing word boundaries and outputs a set of objective measurements suitable for statistical analysis. We run ProsodyPro for each audio and TextGrid pair of sentences to generate the prosodic analysis files. See Table 2 for the list of analyses performed by ProsodyPro (Information taken from ProsodyPro webpage[4]).

The TextGrid file with word boundaries is produced by sending the sentence audio and transcript to the word-aligner software and then converting the alignment information in XML into TextGrid format. Having word boundaries makes it possible to align continuous prosodic parameters (such as pitch contour) with the words in the sentence.

3.3 Parallel sentence alignment

This stage involves the creation of the parallel data from two monolingual data obtained from different audio and subtitle pairs of the same movie. The goal is to find the corresponding sentence s_2 in language 2, given a sentence s_1 in language 1. For each s_1 with timestamps (s_{s_1}, e_{s_1}), s_2 is searched within a sliding window among sentences that start in the time interval $[s_{s_1} - 5, s_{s_1} + 5]$. Among candidate sentences within the range, the most similar to s_1 is found by first translating s_1 to language 2 and then choosing the $\{s_1, s_2\}$ pair that gives the best translation similarity measure above a certain threshold. For translation, the *Yandex Translate* API[5] and for similarity measure the *Meteor* library (Denkowski and Lavie, 2014) is used.

4 Obtained Corpus and Discussion

We have tested our methodology on three movies, which we retrieved from the University Library: *The Man Who Knew Too Much* (1956), *Slow West* (2015) and *The Perfect Guy* (2015). The movies are originally in English, but also have dubbed Spanish audio. English and Spanish subtitles were

[4]http://www.homepages.ucl.ac.uk/~uclyyix/ProsodyPro/

[5]https://tech.yandex.com/translate/

ProsodyPro output file	Description
rawf0	Raw f0 contour in Hz
f0	Smoothed f0 with trimming algorithm (Hz)
smoothf0	Smoothed f0 with triangular window (Hz)
semitonef0	f0 contour in semitones
samplef0	f0 values at fixed time intervals (Hz)
f0velocity	First derivative of f0
means	f0, intensity and velocity parameters (mean, max, min) for each word
normtimef0	Constant number of f0 values for each word
normtimeIntensity	Constant number of intensity values for each word

Table 2: Some of the files generated by ProsodyPro.

acquired from the *opensubtitles* webpage[6].

At the time of the submission, we have automatically extracted 2603 sentences in English and 1963 sentences in Spanish summing up to 80 and 49 minutes of audio respectively and annotated with prosodic parameters. 1328 of these sentences were aligned to create our current parallel bilingual corpora. We are in the process of expanding our dataset.

Due to the copyright on the movies, we are unable to distribute the corpus that we extracted. However, using our software, it is easy for any researcher to compile a corpus on their own. For testing purposes, English and Spanish subtitles and audio of a small portion of the movie *The Man Who Knew Too Much*, as well as the parallel data extracted with this methodology are made available on the github page of the project.

Movie ID	# sentences extracted (eng / spa)	# sentences aligned (parallel)
slow.west	414 / 315	237
tmwktm	1429 / 813	599
perfect.guy	760 / 835	492
TOTAL	2603 / 1963	1328

Table 3: Process results for three movies.

Lang.	# subtitle entries	# sentence end marks	# sentences extracted
eng	1743	1681	1429
spa	1266	1613	813

Table 4: Sentence extraction statistics in English (original audio) and Spanish (dubbed audio) of the movie *The Man Who Knew Too Much*.

Table 3 lists the number of monolingual and

parallel sentences obtained from the three movies so far. We observe that the number of Spanish sentences extracted in stage 2 is sometimes lower than the number of English sentences. This is mainly because of the translation difference between the Spanish subtitles and the dubbed Spanish audio. Subtitles in languages other than the original language of the movie do not always correspond with the transcript used in dubbing. If the audio and the text obtained from the subtitle do not match, the word aligner software performs poorly and that sentence is skipped. This results in fewer number of extracted sentences in dubbed languages of the movie. Table 4 shows more in detail the effect of this. Poor audio-text alignment results in loss of 15.0% of the sentences in original audio, whereas in dubbed audio this loss increases to 49.6%.

Another major effect on detection of sentences is the background noise. This again interferes with the performance of the word aligner software. But since samples with less background noise is desired for a speech database, elimination of these samples is not considered as a problem.

5   Conclusions and Future Work

We have presented a methodology for the extraction of multimodal speech, text and prosody parallel corpora from dubbed movies. Movies contain large samples of conversational speech, which makes the obtained corpus especially useful for speech-to-speech translation applications. It is also useful for other research fields such as large comparative linguistic and prosodic studies.

As long as we have access to a matching pair of audio and subtitles of movies, the corpora obtained can be extended as a multilingual speech parallel corpora adaptable to any language pair. Moreover, it is an open-source tool and it can be

---

adapted to any other prosodic feature extraction module in order to obtain a customized prosody parallel corpus for any specific application. The code to extract multilingual parallel corpora together with a processed sample movie excerpt is open source and available to use[7] under the GNU General Public License[8].

As future work, we plan to extend our corpus in size and make the parallel prosodic parameters available online. We also plan to replace the proprietary word aligner tool we are using with an open source alternative with better precision and speed.

Acknowledgments

We would like to thank Alicia Burga for giving the initial idea of this work. This work is part of the KRISTINA project, which has received funding from the *European Union's Horizon 2020 Research and Innovation Programme* under the Grant Agreement number 645012. The second author is partially funded by the Spanish Ministry of Economy, Industry and Competitiveness through the *Ramón y Cajal* program.

References

Pablo D. Agüero, Jordi Adell, and Antonio Bonafonte. 2006. Prosody generation for speech-to-speech translation. In *International Conference on Acoustics, Speech, and Signal Processing (ICASSP)*. IEEE, volume 1, pages 557–560.

Khalid Almeman, Mark Lee, and Ali Abdulrahman Almiman. 2013. Multi dialect Arabic speech parallel corpora. In *1st International Conference on Communications, Signal Processing, and their Applications (ICCSPA)*. IEEE, pages 1–6.

Gopala Krishna Anumanchipalli, Luís C. Oliveira, and Alan W. Black. 2012. Intent transfer in speech-to-speech machine translation. In *Spoken Language Technology (SLT) Workshop*. IEEE, pages 153–158.

Claudio Bendazzoli and Annalisa Sandrelli. 2005. An approach to corpus-based interpreting studies: developing EPIC (European Parliament Interpreting Corpus). In *MuTra 2005–Challenges of Multidimensional Translation*. pages 1–12.

Paul Boersma and David Weenink. 2001. Praat, a system for doing phonetics by computer. *Glot International* 5(9/10):341–345.

Michael Denkowski and Alon Lavie. 2014. Meteor universal: Language specific translation evaluation for any target language. In *Proceedings of the EACL Workshop on Statistical Machine Translation*.

Christian Federmann and William D. Lewis. 2016. Microsoft Speech Language Translation (MSLT) corpus: The IWSLT 2016 release for English, French and German. In *International Workshop on Spoken Language Translation*.

Einav Itamar and Alon Itai. 2008. Using movie subtitles for creating a large-scale bilingual corpora. In *6th International Conference on Language Resources and Evaluation (LREC)*.

Pierre Lison and Jörg Tiedemann. 2016. OpenSubtitles2016: Extracting large parallel corpora from movie and TV subtitles. In *10th International Conference on Language Resources and Evaluation (LREC 2016)*. pages 923–929.

Robert S. Melvin, Win May, Shrikanth S. Narayanan, Panayiotis G. Georgiou, and Shadi Ganjavi. 2004. Creation of a doctor-patient dialogue corpus using standardized patients. In *4th International Conference on Language Resources and Evaluation (LREC)*.

Vivek Kumar Rangarajan Sridhar, Srinivas Bangalore, and Shrikanth S. Narayanan. 2008. Factored translation models for enriching spoken language translation with prosody. In *Interspeech*. pages 2723–2726.

Andreas Tsiartas, Prasanta Ghosh, Panayiotis G Georgiou, and Shrikanth Narayanan. 2011. Bilingual audio-subtitle extraction using automatic segmentation of movie audio. In *International Conference on Acoustics, Speech and Signal Processing (ICASSP)*. IEEE, pages 5624–5627.

Mirjam Wester. 2010. The EMIME Bilingual Database. Technical report, The University of Edinburgh.

Yi Xu. 2013. ProsodyPro — A Tool for Large-scale Systematic Prosody Analysis. In *Tools and Resources for the Analysis of Speech Prosody (TRASP 2013)*. pages 7–10.

---

[7] https://github.com/TalnUPF/movie2parallelDB
[8] http://www.gnu.org/licenses

A parallel collection of clinical trials in Portuguese and English

Mariana Neves

Hasso Plattner Institute at University of Potsdam
August Bebel Strasse 88, Potsdam 14482 Germany
mariana.neves@hpi.de

Abstract

Parallel collections of documents are crucial resources for training and evaluating machine translation (MT) systems. Even though large collections are available for certain domains and language pairs, these are still scarce in the biomedical domain. We developed a parallel corpus of clinical trials in Portuguese and English. The documents are derived from the Brazilian Clinical Trials Registry and the corpus currently contains a total of 1188 documents. In this paper, we describe the corpus construction and discuss the quality of the translation and the sentence alignment that we obtained.

1 Introduction

It is well know that parallel collections of documents are valuable resources for training, tuning and evaluating machine translation (MT) tools. These are an alternative to relying on expensive bilingual dictionaries. However, parallel documents are only available for some particular languages and domains, e.g, (Koehn, 2005). Additionally, building such a corpus usually requires manual translation of documents from one language to another, which is an expensive and time-consuming task.

Even though many corpora are available for a variety of domains and languages (e.g., news text[1]), these are still scarce for biomedicine. However, domain-specific documents are indeed necessary in order to address the complexity and variety of the biomedical terminology.

Most of medical documents cannot be made freely available due to privacy issues, as it is the case of discharge summaries. Furthermore, many of such documents are only available in one language. On the other hand, scientific publications are a rich source of biomedical terminology, but these are mostly available only in the English language. Even though there has been previous work on biomedical MT using titles and abstracts of scientific publications (Jimeno Yepes et al., 2013; Wu Cuijun et al., 2011), few document collections are currently available for training MT systems. As far as we know, there are two comprehensive collections for parallel documents to support biomedical MT: (i) the UFAL Medical corpus[2] that has a focus on medicine and gathers documents derived from three research projects (KConnect, Khresmoi and HimL); and (ii) the Scielo corpus (Neves et al., 2016), which includes comparable scientific publications from a Latin American database. Both collections have supported previous MT challenges (Bojar et al., 2014, 2016).

Clinical trials are important source of information of the biomedical terminology and could be used to support training of MT systems. Such documents are the standard procedures to evaluate the effectiveness of a treatment, therapy or medication for a particular disease or ailment[3]. The aim of these documents is to recruit patients to take part on the studies, usually though invitation from the physicians. Therefore, they are usually publicly available in order to increase their visibility, for instance, in the ClinicalTrials.org database[4]. Clinical trial documents usually include information about the purpose of the trial, details of the procedure, conditions that the patient should meet, i.e., inclusion and exclusion criteria, as well as pri-

---

[1] `http://www.statmt.org/wmt17/translation-task.html`

[2] `https://ufal.mff.cuni.cz/ufal_medical_corpus`

[3] `https://www.nhlbi.nih.gov/studies/clinicaltrials`

[4] `http://clinicaltrials.gov`

Proceedings of the 10th Workshop on Building and Using Comparable Corpora, pages 36–40,
Vancouver, Canada, August 3, 2017. ©2017 Association for Computational Linguistics

mary or secondary outcomes. Nevertheless, most clinical trials seem to be available in only one language, which undermine their use for MT systems.

We present the first parallel corpus of clinical trials. The documents are derived from the Brazilian Clinical Trials Registry (Registro Brasileiro de Ensaios Clínicos - ReBEC)[5]. The database currently contains 1314 registered trials (as of April 21, 2017). Documents in ReBEC are composed of many fields, such as the scientific title, the description of the intervention, inclusion criteria, exclusion criteria, primary outcomes and secondary outcomes (cf. Figure 1). For all documents, most of these fields are available in English and Portuguese and translation has probably been carried out by the responsible of the trial. The trials can be easily downloaded from the web site and are allowed be redistributed (confirmed by personal communication via e-mail).

We describe the construction of our corpus, which included parsing the XML files and performing sentence splitting, tokenization, automatic sentence alignment and manual checking the aligned sentences. We compiled a total of 1188 parallel documents and we believe that this resource can support training, testing or tuning MT systems. The documents are available at `https://github.com/biomedical-translation-corpora/rebec`. Given the scarce number of biomedical resources for MT, additional data is of much value in the field.

2 Corpus construction

In this section, we describe the procedure to create a parallel corpus of clinical trials. Our workflow was inspired in the one carried out for the Scielo corpus (Neves et al., 2016), even though we used different NLP components and skipped the crawling step, which is not necessary in ReBEC.

Data download. Users can easily download clinical trials from ReBEC by simply selecting some clinical trials from a list and by clicking on the check-box. It is possible to select all trials on the page by clicking on the corresponding checkbox. Selected trials are then exported to a Open-Trials XML file. The only limitation is that up to ten trials are presented per page. Therefore, we had to repeat this procedure many times un-

til we had downloaded their totality (120 files as of January 4th). We did not distinguish between the many types or topics in the trials, in order to obtain a dataset as general-purpose as possible.

OpenTrials XML Parsing. We parsed the OpenTrials XML using some procedures developed in Java. We considered only the following eight fields when parsing the XML file: (a) the trial identifier (element "trial_id"); (b) the public tittle of the trial (element "public_title"); (c) the scientific title of the trial (element "scientific_title"); (d) the interventions to be carried out in the trial (element "interventions"); (e) the inclusion criteria for taking part in the trial (element "inclusion_criteria"); (f) the exclusion criteria for not participating in the trial (element "exclusion_criteria"); (g) the primary outcome of the trial (element "primary_outcome"); (h) the secondary outcome of the trial (element "secondary_outcome").

The identification of the language is not straightforward in the OpenTrials XML format. For some fields, it is identified by the attribute "language" or "lang" in some tags, and sometimes by specific tags, such as "translation" or "outcome_translation". Nevertheless, it is always possible to identify the language of the text in each field, and therefore, it is not necessary to make use of language recognition tools.

We exported the above fields into the the BioC format (Comeau et al., 2013), a standard XML format in the biomedical NLP community. This XML format contains one "passage" tag for each of the above fields, while the name of the field and the language are informed using the so-called "infons" in the BioC format (cf. Figure 2). We tried to position the passages in the same order as they occur in the XML format in order to reduce possible errors in the automatic alignment step (cf. below) and we followed the same notation defined in the Scielo corpus (Neves et al., 2016). We obtained a total of 1188 documents.

Sentence splitting. This step consists on splitting the sentences in each of the passages, i.e., each of the fields of the trials. This is a necessary step for later align the documents sentence by sentence. We used the OpenNLP[6] tool for sentence splitting and utilized the corresponding models for English and Portuguese.

---

[5]`http://www.ensaiosclinicos.gov.br/`

[6]`https://opennlp.apache.org/`

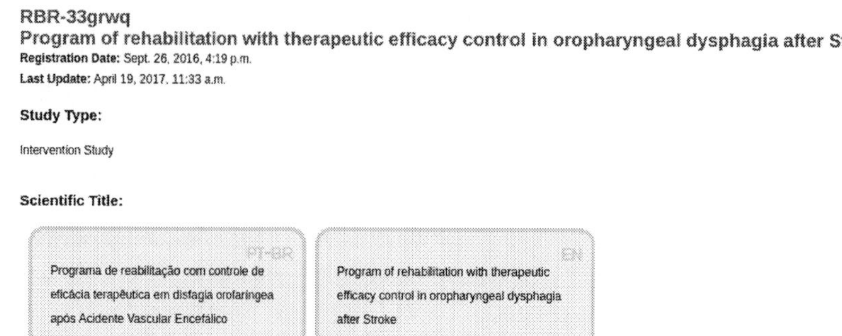

Figure 1: Screen-shot of a clinical trial in ReBEC.

```
- <collection>
    <source/>
    <date/>
    <key/>
  - <document>
      <id>RBR-2cxrpp</id>
    - <passage>
        <infon key="seq-section">1</infon>
        <infon key="section">public_title</infon>
        <infon key="lang">en</infon>
        <offset>-1</offset>
      - <text>
          Effect of Two Kinds of Therapy on Women with Patellofemoral
          Pain Syndrome
        </text>
      </passage>
    - <passage>
        <infon key="seq-section">2</infon>
        <infon key="section">scientific_title</infon>
        <infon key="lang">en</infon>
        <offset>-1</offset>
      - <text>
          Effects of Lumbo-pelvic Stabilization Training on Women with
          Patellofemoral Pain Syndrome
        </text>
      </passage>
```

Figure 2: Screen-shot of one of the document in the BioC XML format.

Sentence alignment. Similar to the work of (Neves et al., 2016), we aligned the sentences using the Geometric Mapping and Alignment (GMA) tool[7]. Sentence alignment is a necessary step for many MT tools (Sennrich and Volk, 2011). In this work, our aim was to align the sentences to further check the quality of the translation in the next step. Given the long length of the documents, a validation based on the whole document would not be feasible using the current available validation tools, e.g., Appraise (Federmann, 2010).

We converted each document to their .axis file format using scripts available in the GMA tool. In a next step, we aligned the sentences using the default parameters of the tool. We only had to inform a list of stopwords for each language and we use the following for Portuguese[8] and English[9].

Quality checking. We randomly selected a sample of 50 clinical trials to manually check the quality of the alignment, translation and sentence splitting and obtained a total of 891 items (pairs). We utilized the Appraise tool[10] (Federmann, 2010), which is freely available. Appraise includes various tasks to manually validate the quality of translations. We used the "Quality Checking" task which consists of showing the source sentence(s) (i.e., in Portuguese), and the corresponding aligned translation sentences (i.e. English). More than one sentence might be shown for any of the two languages depending on the output of the alignment tool. The validation was carried out by the author who is a native speaker of Brazilian Portuguese. Similar to (Neves et al., 2016), we adopted five options when checking the items, as described below:

- OK: correct text alignment, i.e., the English translation is a correct translation of the Portuguese source.

- Source>Target: there is more information in the source (Portuguese) text than in the translation (English) text.

- Target>Source: there is more information in the translation (English) text than in the source (Portuguese) text.

- Overlap: there is some overlap between both text but also information which are just present in each on of them.

- No alignment: wrong alignment of the sentences.

---

[7] http://nlp.cs.nyu.edu/GMA/

[8] http://www.linguateca.pt/chave/stopwords/chave.MF300.txt

[9] http://www.textfixer.com/tutorials/common-english-words.txt

[10] https://github.com/cfedermann/Appraise

Language	Sentences	Tokens
EN	23,843	625,881
PT	23,666	665,325

Table 1: Statistics on the size of the collection of parallel clinical trials.

At the end of the validation process, Appraise provides statistics for the chosen options and allows the user to export the results for further analysis.

3 Results and discussion

In this section we present statistics on the corpus and the results of the manual evaluation of a sample of documents. Table 1 shows statistics on the size of the collection of clinical trials for each language. The number of tokens is based on the OpenNLP tool for both languages using the corresponding available models. Even though the collection is much smaller that the ones available for Portuguese/English and Spanish/English in the Scielo corpus, it is larger than the the one available for French/English in the same corpus. Additionally, we have a higher number of documents than some of the collections available in the UFAL Medical corpus.

Table 2 shows the results of the validation of the sample of 50 clinical trials. A total of 67% of the items were correctly aligned, while overlaps and text in one language containing more information than in the other language were rather rare (around 4% in total). The "Target >Source" or "Source >Target" options were selected even when difference was minimal, such as in one case in which the English translation contained the expression "24-hour", which was not present in the Portuguese version. Some of these mistakes were also due to two sentences in one language being aligned to just one in the other language, while the corresponding second sentence was placed in the next alignment block, i.e., an error caused by the sentence alignment step.

However, in contrast to the results reported for the Scielo corpus, we obtained a much higher number (and percentage) of wrong alignments (the "No alignment" option). During validation, we noticed a high number of empty sentences, which is the result of empty lines in the original files. This mistake accounts for 27 of the wrong alignments, however, this is still only around 1/5 of the total errors for this type.

Result	No. items (%)
OK	597 (67.00%)
Source>Target	25 (2.81%)
Target>Source	15 (1.68%)
Overlap	4 (0.45%)
No alignment	250 (28.06%)
total	891 (100%)

Table 2: Results from the manual validation of the sample of 50 clinical trials using the Appraise tool (Quality Checking task).

Some wrong alignments were due to mistakes in the sentence splitting components. For instance, one Portuguese sentence ending on "[...] durante 45 minutos, num total de 16 sesses." was aligned to the English sentence "45 minutes, totaling 16 sessions.". The English sentence was mistakenly split before the token "45", and the rest of this sentence was placed on the previous alignment block. There is no clear reason on why the OpenNLP tool split the sentence at this particular point for the English sentence, but not for the corresponding Portuguese sentence.

Finally, many wrong alignments were probably due to errors from the GMA tool. In many cases, for no clear reason, sentences from one field were aligned to sentences from the adjoining field. Indeed, our input data to GMA does not distinguish the boundaries between the fields.

In general, the English translation is of good quality, although some lexical and grammar errors did occur. However, cases in which the English translation was particularly bad were rather rare, e.g., the sentence "Secondary outcomes are expected not".

4 Conclusions and future work

We presented the construction of the first parallel collection of clinical trials. Our document collection is not particularly small, in comparison with previous works, however, the quality of the alignment that we obtained was rather low. To overcome this problem, we believe that a better alignment could be obtained by carrying it out for each field separately, instead of the complete document. However, given that some fields appear more than once and in no particular order in the file, precisely extracting the fields is not a straightforward task. Further, we plan to try other sentence alignment tools, besides the GMA tool, and analyze the suitability of the corpus for training biomedical MT systems. Finally, our future versions of the corpus will also include additional fields to the ones considered here.

Acknowledgments

We would like to thank ReBEC for granting us permission to redistribute the clinical trials.

References

Ondrej Bojar, Christian Buck, Christian Federmann, Barry Haddow, Philipp Koehn, Johannes Leveling, Christof Monz, Pavel Pecina, Matt Post, Herve Saint-Amand, Radu Soricut, Lucia Specia, and Aleš Tamchyna. 2014. Findings of the 2014 workshop on statistical machine translation. In *Proceedings of the Ninth Workshop on Statistical Machine Translation*. Association for Computational Linguistics, Baltimore, Maryland, USA, pages 12–58.

Ondrej Bojar, Rajen Chatterjee, Christian Federmann, Yvette Graham, Barry Haddow, Matthias Huck, Antonio Jimeno Yepes, Philipp Koehn, Varvara Logacheva, Christof Monz, Matteo Negri, Aurelie Neveol, Mariana Neves, Martin Popel, Matt Post, Raphael Rubino, Carolina Scarton, Lucia Specia, Marco Turchi, Karin Verspoor, and Marcos Zampieri. 2016. Findings of the 2016 conference on machine translation. In *Proceedings of the First Conference on Machine Translation (WMT16) at the Conference of the Association of Computational Linguistics*, pages 131–198.

Donald C. Comeau, Rezarta Islamaj Doan, Paolo Ciccarese, Kevin Bretonnel Cohen, Martin Krallinger, Florian Leitner, Zhiyong Lu, Yifan Peng, Fabio Rinaldi, Manabu Torii, Alfonso Valencia, Karin Verspoor, Thomas C. Wiegers, Cathy H. Wu, and W. John Wilbur. 2013. Bioc: a minimalist approach to interoperability for biomedical text processing. *Database* 2013.

Christian Federmann. 2010. Appraise: An open-source toolkit for manual phrase-based evaluation of translations. In Nicoletta Calzolari, Khalid Choukri, Bente Maegaard, Joseph Mariani, Jan Odijk, Stelios Piperidis, Mike Rosner, and Daniel Tapias, editors, *LREC*. European Language Resources Association.

Antonio Jimeno Yepes, Elise Prieur-Gaston, and Aurelie Neveol. 2013. Combining medline and publisher data to create parallel corpora for the automatic translation of biomedical text. *BMC Bioinformatics* 14(1):146.

Philipp Koehn. 2005. Europarl: A Parallel Corpus for Statistical Machine Translation. In *Conference Proceedings: the tenth Machine Translation Summit*. AAMT, AAMT, Phuket, Thailand, pages 79–86.

Mariana Neves, Antonio Jimeno Yepes, and Aurlie Nvol. 2016. The scielo corpus: a parallel corpus of scientific publications for biomedicine. In Nicoletta Calzolari (Conference Chair), Khalid Choukri, Thierry Declerck, Sara Goggi, Marko Grobelnik, Bente Maegaard, Joseph Mariani, Helene Mazo, Asuncion Moreno, Jan Odijk, and Stelios Piperidis, editors, *Proceedings of the Tenth International Conference on Language Resources and Evaluation (LREC 2016)*. European Language Resources Association (ELRA), Paris, France.

R Sennrich and M Volk. 2011. Iterative, mt-based sentence alignment of parallel texts. In *NODALIDA 2011, Nordic Conference of Computational Linguistics*.

Wu Cuijun, Xia Fei, Deleger Louise, and Solti Imre. 2011. Statistical Machine Translation for Biomedical Text: Are We There Yet? *AMIA Annual Symposium Proceedings* 2011:1290–1299.

Weighted Set-Theoretic Alignment of Comparable Sentences

Andoni Azpeitia and **Thierry Etchegoyhen** and **Eva Martínez Garcia**
Vicomtech-IK4
Mikeletegi Pasalekua, 57
Donostia / San Sebastian, Gipuzkoa, Spain
{aazpeitia, tetchegoyhen, emartinez}@vicomtech.org

Abstract

This article presents the STACC$_w$ system for the BUCC 2017 shared task on parallel sentence extraction from comparable corpora. The original STACC approach, based on set-theoretic operations over bags of words, had been previously shown to be efficient and portable across domains and alignment scenarios. We describe an extension of this approach with a new weighting scheme and show that it provides significant improvements on the datasets provided for the shared task.

1 Introduction

Parallel corpora are an essential resource for the development of multilingual natural language processing applications, in particular statistical and neural machine translation (Brown et al., 1990; Bahdanau et al., 2014). Since the professional translations that are necessary to build quality bitexts are expensive and time-consuming, the exploitation of monolingual corpora that address similar topics, known as comparable corpora, has been extensively explored in the last two decades (Munteanu and Marcu, 2005; Sharoff et al., 2016).

A critical part of the process when building parallel resources from comparable data is the alignment of sentences in monolingual corpora. Over the years, several methods have been developed and evaluated for this task, including maximum likelihood (Zhao and Vogel, 2002), suffix trees (Munteanu and Marcu, 2002), binary classification (Munteanu and Marcu, 2005), cosine similarity (Fung and Cheung, 2004), reference metrics over statistical machine translations (Abdul-Rauf and Schwenk, 2009; Sarikaya et al., 2009), and feature-based approaches (Stefănescu et al., 2012; Smith et al., 2010), among others.

For comparable sentence alignment, we followed the STACC approach in (Etchegoyhen et al., 2016; Etchegoyhen and Azpeitia, 2016), which is based on seed lexical translations, simple set expansion operations and the Jaccard similarity coefficient (Jaccard, 1901). This method has been shown to outperform state-of-the-art alternatives on a large range of alignment tasks and provides a simple yet effective procedure that can be applied across domains and corpora with minimal adaptation and deployment costs.

In this paper, we describe STACC$_w$, an extension of the approach with a word weighting scheme, and show that it provides significant improvements on the datasets provided for the BUCC 2017 shared task, while maintaining the portability of the original approach.

2 STACC

STACC is an approach to sentence similarity based on expanded lexical sets and Jaccard similarity, whose main goal is to provide a portable and efficient alignment mechanism for comparable sentences. The similarity score is computed as follows.

Let s_i and s_j be two tokenised and truecased sentences in languages l_1 and l_2, respectively, S_i the set of tokens in s_i, S_j the set of tokens in s_j, T_{ij} the set of lexical translations into l_2 for all tokens in S_i, and T_{ji} the set of lexical translations into l_1 for all tokens in S_j.

Lexical translations are initially computed from sentences s_i and s_j by retaining the k-best translations for each word, if any, as determined by IBM models.[1] Lexical translations are selected according to the ranking provided by the precomputed lexical probabilities, without using the

---

[1]Translation tables are generated with the GIZA++ toolkit (Och and Ney, 2003).

Proceedings of the 10th Workshop on Building and Using Comparable Corpora, pages 41–45,
Vancouver, Canada, August 3, 2017. ©2017 Association for Computational Linguistics

actual probability values in the computation of similarity. The sets T_{ij} and T_{ji} that comprise the k-best lexical translations are then expanded by means of two operations:

1. For each element in the set difference $T'_{ij} = T_{ij} - S_j$ (respectively $T'_{ji} = T_{ji} - S_i$), and each element in S_j (respectively S_i), if both elements share a common prefix with minimal length of more than n characters, the prefix is added to both sets. This longest common prefix matching strategy is meant to capture morphological variation via minimal computation.

2. Numbers and capitalised truecased tokens not found in the translation tables are added to the expanded translation sets. This operation addresses named entities, which are strong indicators of potential alignment given their low relative frequency and are likely to be missing from translation tables trained on different domains.

No additional operations are performed on the created sets, and in particular no filtering is applied, with punctuation and functional words kept alongside content words in the final sets. With source and target sets as defined here, the STACC similarity score is then computed as in Equation 1:

$$stacc(s_i, s_j) = \frac{\frac{|T_{ij} \cap S_j|}{|T_{ij} \cup S_j|} + \frac{|T_{ji} \cap S_i|}{|T_{ji} \cup S_i|}}{2} \quad (1)$$

Similarity is thus defined as the average of the Jaccard similarity coefficients obtained between sentence token sets and expanded lexical translations in both directions.

For scenarios where the alignment space is large, target sentences are first indexed using the Lucene search engine[2] and retrieved by building a query over the expanded translation sets created from each source sentence. This strategy drastically reduces the computational load, at the cost of missing some correct alignment pairs. In this mode, one of the two corpora is set as source and the other as target, retrieving n target alignment candidates for each source sentence. Similarity is computed over all candidates and a final optimisation process is applied that enforces 1-1 alignments, a process which has been shown to improve the quality of alignments (Etchegoyhen and Azpeitia, 2016).

---

[2]https://lucene.apache.org.

3 Weighted STACC

Although STACC has been shown to outperform competing state-of-the-art approaches on a variety of domains and scenarios (Etchegoyhen and Azpeitia, 2016), it ignores lexical weights and thus assigns equal importance to open-class and function words. Although it makes intuitive sense to assign different weights according to the information provided by each word, adequate lexical weighting for a given task is not straightforward. Standard approaches such as TF-IDF often need to be complemented with stop word lists, which can be large and difficult to determine in agglutinative languages, for instance. Term-based approaches in general might assign weights that are too unbalanced for the task at hand, and termhood might be dependent on building accurate contrastive generic corpora (Gelbukh et al., 2010).

We follow the empirical approach in (Mikolov et al., 2013), where the imbalance between frequent and rare words is controlled by a subsampling formula with two variables: an empirically determined threshold and word frequency. Experiments with their exact weighting scheme did not however provide optimal results for our alignment goals. We opted instead to compute lexical weights according to Equation 2, where $f(w_i)$ is the relative frequency of word w_i and α is a parameter controlling the smoothness of the curve.

$$W(w_i) = \frac{1}{e^{\sqrt{\alpha \cdot f(w_i)}}} \quad (2)$$

Among the methods we tested empirically, this function has properties that fit rather well the original STACC approach. First, since it is bound between zero and one, it preserves the idea that set membership is a fruitful factor to compute similarity. Secondly, it assigns weights close to 1 for most open-class words while not completely discarding functional words,[3] a feature which has provided optimal results in our experiments.

Weighting is computed on each monolingual corpus to be aligned, thus removing any dependence on defining contrastive generic corpora. STACC$_w$ similarity is then computed according to the previously defined equation, except that set membership values of 1 in the original approach are replaced with lexical weights.

---

[3]The most frequent words typically receive a weight around 0.1 in the various distributions we tested.

PAIR	LANG	MONOLINGUAL			GOLD	
		TRAIN	SAMPLE	TEST	TRAIN	SAMPLE
DE-EN	de	413,869	32,593	413,884	9,573	1,037
	en	399,337	40,354	396,534	9,573	1,037
EN-FR	fr	271,874	21,497	276,833	9,080	929
	en	369,810	38,069	373,459	9,080	929

Table 1: Task data statistics (number of sentences)

PAIR	DATA	CORPUS					
		OPENSUBS	MULTIUN	EUROPARL	JRC	TED	GENERIC
DE-EN	Original	11,473,328	103,490	1,776,292	449,818	138,243	*13,941,171*
	Selected	500,000	103,490	500,000	449,818	139,243	*1,692,551*
FR-EN	Original	28,024,360	9,142,161	1,826,770	708,896	153,167	*39,855,354*
	Selected	500,000	500,000	500,000	316,327	153,167	*1,969,494*

Table 2: Generic data (number of sentences)

4 BUCC 2017 Shared Task

The BUCC 2017 shared task on parallel sentence extraction from comparable corpora[4] consists in identifying translation pairs within two sentence-split monolingual corpora. It involves four language pairs, from which we selected French-English and German-English for our participation.

The organisers provided three datasets for each language pair, whose statistics are described in Table 1 for the two language pairs we selected; gold reference pairs were provided for the training and sample sets.

Note that the statistics shown here differ slightly from those of the original data provided by the organisers, as we removed the bilingual duplicates that were found.[5]

4.1 Experimental Settings

Both STACC and STACC$_w$ require lexical translation tables to compute similarity, the only external source of information needed in this approach. In previous work (Etchegoyhen and Azpeitia, 2016), GIZA tables had been created from the JRC corpora only. In order to extend lexical coverage, we opted for a different approach and created generic translation tables from varied corpora.

In each corpus, parallel sentence pairs were first sorted by increasing perplexity scores according to language models trained on the monolingual side of each parallel corpus, where the score was taken to be the mean of source and target perplexities. A portion of each corpus was then selected to compose the final corpus, with an upper selection bound taken to be either the median average perplexity score or the top n pairs if selecting up to median perplexity would result in over representing the corpus. Table 2 describes the number of sentence pairs selected for each language pair, the lexical translation tables being extracted from the GENERIC datasets.[6]

Regarding hyper-parameters, k-best lexical translations were limited to a maximum of 4 and the minimal prefix length for longest common prefix matching was set to 4. Lucene indexing was based on words with length of 4 or more characters, and a maximum of 100 candidates were retrieved for each source sentence. For each language pair, English was set to be the target language. We experimented with different values of α to control the smoothness of the weighting function and different values for the alignment threshold th used to discard low-confidence alignments.

Since up to three different runs could be submitted for the task, we prepared three variants of the system, where parameters α and th were set according to the best f-measure, precision and recall scores, respectively, obtained on the training set.[7]

Each of these variants was submitted to the task, in order to evaluate the behaviour of our system when targeting for precision, recall and f-measure. Although not submitted to the shared task, the original STACC method was also evaluated on the train and sample sets.

---

[4]https://comparable.limsi.fr/bucc2017/bucc2017-task.html

[5]There were 7 and 1 duplicates in the train and sample sets, respectively, for DE-EN, and 6 in the FR-EN train set.

[6]All original corpora were downloaded from the OPUS repository (Tiedemann, 2012): http://opus.lingfil.uu.se/; the upper bound n was set to 500,000 after considering the relative weights of the available corpora.

[7]We identify these variants with F, P and R upperscripts in the tables.

DATASET	SYSTEM	α	th	LUCENE	P	R	F
TRAIN	STACC_w^F	250	0.17	98.50	86.99	79.96	**83.33**
TRAIN	STACC_w^P	250	0.18	98.50	**90.89**	73.41	81.23
TRAIN	STACC_w^R	250	0.16	98.50	80.21	**85.55**	82.79
TRAIN	STACC	_	0.23	98.50	79.26	69.16	73.87
SAMPLE	STACC_w^F	100	0.16	99.04	95.46	91.32	**93.35**
SAMPLE	STACC_w^P	100	0.17	99.04	**97.95**	87.75	92.57
SAMPLE	STACC_w^R	100	0.15	99.04	88.27	**93.64**	90.88
SAMPLE	STACC	_	0.22	99.04	91.84	80.33	85.70
TEST	STACC_w^F	250	0.17	98.63	88.15	79.75	**83.74**
TEST	STACC_w^P	250	0.18	98.63	**92.10**	73.16	81.55
TEST	STACC_w^R	250	0.16	98.63	81.93	**85.35**	83.60

Table 3: Results for DE-EN

DATASET	SYSTEM	α	th	LUCENE	P	R	F
TRAIN	STACC_w^F	250	0.16	96.84	78.43	79.23	**78.83**
TRAIN	STACC_w^P	250	0.17	96.84	**84.36**	73.40	78.50
TRAIN	STACC_w^R	250	0.15	96.84	68.51	**83.83**	75.40
TRAIN	STACC	_	0.23	96.84	72.69	63.12	67.57
SAMPLE	STACC_w^F	500	0.14	99.46	90.51	91.39	**90.95**
SAMPLE	STACC_w^P	500	0.15	99.46	**93.74**	86.98	90.23
SAMPLE	STACC_w^R	500	0.13	99.46	83.13	**93.33**	87.93
SAMPLE	STACC	_	0.22	99.46	89.36	75.03	81.57
TEST	STACC_w^F	250	0.16	96.81	80.41	78.52	**79.46**
TEST	STACC_w^P	250	0.17	96.81	**87.08**	72.89	79.35
TEST	STACC_w^R	250	0.15	96.81	69.82	**83.14**	75.90

Table 4: Results for FR-EN

4.2 Results

Results on all datasets are shown in Tables 3 and 4, along with the parameters used for each dataset and the percentage of correct candidates retrieved via Lucene indexing and search. On the test sets, our system competed with four other systems in FR-EN and our three submitted variants obtained the best results on all three metrics; for DE-EN, there were no other competing systems.

Given the nature of the evaluation, where not all gold parallel sentences are known, pairs identified as false positives may actually be correct alignments.[8] The results shown here are therefore minimum values and the already high scores achieved by our approach were thus quite satisfactory.

Overall, STACC_w improves significantly over its non-weighted variant on the training and sample datasets, with improvements of around 10 points in f-measure on the training and sample sets. On the smaller sample sets, the accuracy of the alignments was naturally higher, reaching f-measure minimum scores above the 90% mark.

As expected, each variant of the system was better on the measure it was meant to optimise via adjustments of the alignment threshold.

An interesting additional result, not shown in the tables, is the weak impact of the hyper-parameter α: between 100 and 500, the scores were marginally different; only values markedly outside this range gave worse results. These results were consistent for both training and sample sets, showing that the weighting function appears not to need corpus-specific adjustments for this parameter, a welcome result on portability grounds.

5 Conclusion

We described STACC_w, a weighted set-theoretic alignment method to extract parallel sentences from comparable corpora, which was the top ranked system in the BUCC 2017 shared task on the datasets where it competed with other systems and achieved high minimum value scores across the board. Our approach features generic lexical translation tables, Jaccard similarity over simple expanded translation sets and a generic word weighting scheme. This method improved significantly over the previous non-weighted approach on the provided training and sample datasets, while maintaining its main goals of portability, efficiency and ease of deployment.

---

[8] A quick manual evaluation of a sample of false positives confirmed that many were in fact correct alignments.

Acknowledgments

This work was partially funded by the Spanish Ministry of Economy and Competitiveness and the Department of Economic Development and Competitiveness of the Basque Government through the AdapTA (RTC-2015-3627-7) and TRADIN (IG-2015/0000347) projects. We would like to thank MondragonLingua Translation & Communication as coordinator of these projects and the four anonymous reviewers for their helpful feedback and suggestions.

References

Sadaf Abdul-Rauf and Holger Schwenk. 2009. On the use of comparable corpora to improve SMT performance. In *Proceedings of the 12th Conference of the European Chapter of the Association for Computational Linguistics*. Association for Computational Linguistics, Stroudsburg, PA, USA, EACL '09, pages 16–23.

Dzmitry Bahdanau, Kyunghyun Cho, and Yoshua Bengio. 2014. Neural machine translation by jointly learning to align and translate. *arXiv:1409.0473* .

Peter F Brown, John Cocke, Stephen A Della Pietra, Vincent J Della Pietra, Fredrick Jelinek, John D Lafferty, Robert L Mercer, and Paul S Roossin. 1990. A statistical approach to machine translation. *Computational linguistics* 16(2):79–85.

Thierry Etchegoyhen and Andoni Azpeitia. 2016. Set-Theoretic Alignment for Comparable Corpora. In *Proceedings of the 54th Annual Meeting of the Association for Computational Linguistics, ACL 2016, August 7-12, 2016, Berlin, Germany*. volume 1: Long Papers, pages 2009–2018.

Thierry Etchegoyhen, Andoni Azpeitia, and Naiara Pérez. 2016. Exploiting a Large Strongly Comparable Corpus. In *Proceedings of the Tenth International Conference on Language Resources and Evaluation (LREC 2016)*. European Language Resources Association (ELRA), Paris, France.

Pascale Fung and Percy Cheung. 2004. Mining Very Non-Parallel Corpora: Parallel Sentence and Lexicon Extraction via Bootstrapping and E.M. In *Proceedings of Empirical Methods in Natural Language Processing*. pages 57–63.

Alexander Gelbukh, Grigori Sidorov, Eduardo Lavin-Villa, and Liliana Chanona-Hernandez. 2010. Automatic term extraction using log-likelihood based comparison with general reference corpus. In *International Conference on Application of Natural Language to Information Systems*. Springer, pages 248–255.

Paul Jaccard. 1901. Distribution de la flore alpine dans le bassin des Dranses et dans quelques régions voisines. *Bulletin de la Société Vaudoise des Sciences Naturelles* 37:241 – 272.

Tomas Mikolov, Ilya Sutskever, Kai Chen, Greg S Corrado, and Jeff Dean. 2013. Distributed representations of words and phrases and their compositionality. In *Advances in neural information processing systems*. pages 3111–3119.

Dragos Stefan Munteanu and Daniel Marcu. 2002. Processing Comparable Corpora With Bilingual Suffix Trees. In *Proceedings of the Conference on Empirical Methods in Natural Language Processing*. Association for Computational Linguistics, pages 289–295.

Dragos Stefan Munteanu and Daniel Marcu. 2005. Improving machine translation performance by exploiting non-parallel corpora. *Computational Linguistics* 31(4):477–504.

Franz Josef Och and Hermann Ney. 2003. A systematic comparison of various statistical alignment models. *Computational linguistics* 29(1):19–51.

Ruhi Sarikaya, Sameer Maskey, R Zhang, Ea-Ee Jan, D Wang, Bhuvana Ramabhadran, and Salim Roukos. 2009. Iterative sentence-pair extraction from quasi-parallel corpora for machine translation. In *Proceedings of InterSpeech*. pages 432–435.

Serge Sharoff, Reinhard Rapp, Pierre Zweigenbaum, and Pascale Fung. 2016. *Building and Using Comparable Corpora*. Springer Publishing Company, Incorporated, 1st edition.

Jason R. Smith, Chris Quirk, and Kristina Toutanova. 2010. Extracting parallel sentences from comparable corpora using document level alignment. In *Human Language Technologies: The 2010 Annual Conference of the North American Chapter of the Association for Computational Linguistics*. Association for Computational Linguistics, Stroudsburg, PA, USA, HLT '10, pages 403–411.

Dan Stefănescu, Radu Ion, and Sabine Hunsicker. 2012. Hybrid parallel sentence mining from comparable corpora. In *Proceedings of the 16th Conference of the European Association for Machine Translation*. pages 137–144.

Jörg Tiedemann. 2012. Parallel data, tools and interfaces in OPUS. In *Proceedings of the 8th Language Resources and Evaluation Conference*. pages 2214–2218.

Bing Zhao and Stephan Vogel. 2002. Adaptive parallel sentences mining from web bilingual news collection. In *Proceedings of the 2002 IEEE International Conference on Data Mining*. IEEE, pages 745–748.

BUCC 2017 Shared Task: a First Attempt Toward a Deep Learning Framework for Identifying Parallel Sentences in Comparable Corpora

Francis Grégoire
RALI - DIRO
Université de Montréal
gregoifr@iro.umontreal.ca

Philippe Langlais
RALI - DIRO
Université de Montréal
felipe@iro.umontreal.ca

Abstract

This paper describes our participation in BUCC 2017 shared task: identifying parallel sentences in comparable corpora. Our goal is to leverage continuous vector representations and distributional semantics with a minimal use of external preprocessing and postprocessing tools. We report experiments that were conducted after transmitting our results.

1 Introduction

Traditional approaches for parallel sentence identification from comparable corpora rely on machine learning models with the use of features measured by statistical machine translation (SMT) systems. Munteanu and Marcu (2005) present how to extract parallel sentences from newspaper articles using general and alignment features to train a binary maximum entropy classifier. Abdul-Rauf and Schwenk (2009) use an SMT-based system on comparable corpora to translate the source language side to detect corresponding parallel sentences on the target language side. While continuous vector representations of words and sentences estimated by neural language models and neural networks (Bengio et al., 2003; Collobert and Weston, 2008) have been successfully applied to a variety of natural language processing tasks, ranging from handwriting generation (Graves, 2013) to machine translation (Sutskever et al., 2014), few efforts have been devoted to parallel sentence identification. Ferrero et al. (2017) successfully use word embeddings for cross-language plagiarism detection, which can be considered a similar task to ours.

The primary objective of our proposed approach is to assess whether we are able to identify parallel sentences using a scalable and flexible method by relying on recent advances in neural language modeling and deep learning architectures to eliminate the need for any domain specific feature engineering. We want to evaluate the feasibility of a model learnt from distributional semantics alone in a "pure" setting by using as few external tools as possible. Our approach can be considered as a first attempt to accomplish the proposed task using a deep learning framework. Our aim is not to attain state-of-the-art performance, but to open interesting directions to enable researchers to advance research with this important task.

In fact, in the following sections we report the approach of our two-day effort to participate on this year's shared task. Due to the short limit of time, we used models pretrained on a standard parallel corpus. The details of our approach will be described elsewhere. In this paper we report what we learned so far and few experiments that were conducted after submitting our results.

2 Approach

2.1 Model

Our model architecture is a bidirectional recurrent neural network with gated recurrent units (Bi-GRU) (Cho et al., 2014) built for both the source language and target language sentences. The Bi-GRU encodes each sentence in both directions to generate two continuous vector representation of the sentence, $\overrightarrow{\mathbf{h}}_i$ and $\overleftarrow{\mathbf{h}}_i$. The forward network processes the input sentence and updates its recurrent state from the first token until the last one. The backward network processes the input sentence in reverse direction. The concatenation of the final recurrent state in both directions is the sentence representation $\mathbf{h}_i = [\overrightarrow{\mathbf{h}}_i ; \overleftarrow{\mathbf{h}}_i]$.

Once both source and target sentence representations have been encoded, $\mathbf{h}_i^S$ and $\mathbf{h}_i^T$, we measure the semantic similarity between the two sentences to estimate the probability that they are par-

Proceedings of the 10th Workshop on Building and Using Comparable Corpora, pages 46–50,
Vancouver, Canada, August 3, 2017. ©2017 Association for Computational Linguistics

allel:

$$p(y_i = 1|\mathbf{h}_i^S, \mathbf{h}_i^T) = \sigma(\mathbf{h}_i^{S\top} \mathbf{M} \mathbf{h}_i^T + b) \quad (1)$$

where $\mathbf{M}$ and b are model parameters, σ is the sigmoid function, $y_i = 1$ if the sentence pair is parallel and $y_i = 0$ otherwise. The model outputs a positive instance if a sentence pair gets a probability score higher than a decision threshold λ:

$$\hat{y}_i = \begin{cases} 1 & \text{if } p(y_i = 1|\mathbf{h}_i^S, \mathbf{h}_i^T) \geq \lambda \\ 0 & \text{otherwise} \end{cases} \quad (2)$$

We train our model by minimizing the cross entropy of our labeled sentence pairs $(\mathbf{x}_i^S, \mathbf{x}_i^T, y_i)$ that we feed in our BiGRU, where $\mathbf{x}_i^S = (\mathbf{w}_{i,1}^S, \ldots, \mathbf{w}_{i,|\mathbf{x}_i^S|}^S)$ is a source sentence and $\mathbf{x}_i^T = (\mathbf{w}_{i,1}^T, \ldots, \mathbf{w}_{i,|\mathbf{x}_i^T|}^T)$ is a target sentence. $\mathbf{w}_{i,t}^S$ and $\mathbf{w}_{i,t}^T$ are the continuous word representation (word embeddings) of the words in the source and target sentences, respectively. We use a parallel corpus made of N parallel sentence pairs $(\mathbf{x}_i^S, \mathbf{x}_i^T)$, for $i \in \{1, \ldots, N\}$. For every pair of parallel sentences we add negative examples by randomly selecting 5 negative sentence pairs $(\mathbf{x}_i^S, \mathbf{x}_j^T)$, for $j \neq i$.

2.2 Candidate filtering

Very often, identifying parallel sentences in comparable corpora is an extremely unbalanced classification task because the number of sentence pairs to be examined is potentially the Cartesian product between sentence pairs in the corpora. This is not an issue for small comparable corpora, e.g. two Wikipedia articles. However, in our case we are given two monolingual corpora of approximately 370,000 and 270,000 sentences, for a potential of $9.99e10$ pairs of sentences to evaluate. To reduce the size and the noise of the candidate sentence pairs, traditional approaches apply candidate filters such as sentence length ratio, bilingual dictionary word overlap, word alignment conditions from SMT and information retrieval systems (Resnik and Smith, 2003; Munteanu and Marcu, 2005; Abdul-Rauf and Schwenk, 2009).

Following our idea to evaluate the feasibility of an approach using only distributional representations, for each sentence we learned its continuous vector representation and created our set of candidate sentence pairs by using the n-best cosine similarity score between each source sentence

and every target sentences. Since we are working with vector representations, doing the Cartesian product is tractable. To estimate the vector representation of each sentence, $\mathbf{s}_i^S$ and $\mathbf{s}_i^T$, we employ a distributional bag-of-words approach where word embeddings have been mapped to a shared vector space, i.e. cross-lingual word embeddings (Gouws et al., 2015). The sentence representation is the normalized sum over the word embeddings present in it:

$$\mathbf{s}_i^S = \frac{\sum_t \mathbf{w}_{i,t}^S}{|\sum_t \mathbf{w}_{i,t}^S|_2} \quad (3)$$

3 Experiments

In this section we present experiments that were conducted after the submission of our results. First, we describe the resources used to perform the shared task, the training settings and the evaluation metrics.

3.1 Dataset

We only participated to the fr-en language pair, making use only of our models pretrained on the Europarl v7 English to French parallel corpus from WMT'15[1]. To create our training set, 500K parallel sentence pairs are randomly selected. The vocabulary sizes range between 103K to 119K for English and 126K to 140K for French depending on the digit preprocessing method (see Section 4.2). We tokenize the dataset with the scripts from Moses[2] and all words are lowercased. Empty sentence pairs are removed.

For the shared task, we replaced all digits with 0 (e.g. 1982→0000).

3.2 Training settings

We use TensorFlow[3] (Abadi et al., 2016) to train our models. The dimension of the BiGRU recurrent state is 200 in each direction with word embeddings of dimension 300. We train our models using a mini-batch size of 128 and Adam optimizer (Kingma and Ba, 2014) with a learning rate of $2e$-4 for a total of 10 epochs. We augment our training examples with new negative examples by sampling 5 negative sentence pairs for each parallel sentence pair. We apply gradient clipping to a value of 5.

---

[1] http://www.statmt.org/wmt15/translation-task.html
[2] https://github.com/moses-smt/mosesdecoder
[3] https://github.com/tensorflow/tensorflow

Cross-lingual word embeddings used for candidate filtering are trained for 10 epochs with the BilBOWA toolkit[4] (Gouws et al., 2015) by using the 2M sentence pairs of Europarl both as monolingual and parallel training data. We use the default parameters with word embedding dimension of 300 and a subsampling rate of value $1e$-4.

3.3 Evaluation metrics

For the evaluation of our models we present the precision, recall and F_1 scores as mentioned on the shared task website[5].

3.4 Details

Candidate filtering To obtain our candidate sentence pairs we apply our n-best cosine similarity filter as described in Section 2.2. For the shared task we applied the filter on the shared task test set, but for the experiment reported here we applied it to the shared task training set. A low n value will result in fewer candidate sentence pairs to evaluate and can be detrimental to the recall score. On the other hand, a high value can lead to an undesirable number of candidate sentence pairs and potentially a lower precision score due to a higher number of false positive examples. We evaluate the loss of parallel sentences in the training set with respect to the value of n.

Digits preprocessing While observing our system's outputs during the shared task we noticed a substantial number of false positive examples due to digits being replaced to 0. Consequently, we analyze our approach by measuring the impact of the following preprocessing choices for training and evaluating our model: (i) keep digits; (ii) replace digits to 0; (iii) remove digits. For this experiment we create validation sets by using the 9,086 pairs of parallel sentences from the shared task training set and adding 50M randomly selected negative sentence pairs. Hence, 0.018% of the sentence pairs are considered parallel.

Model evaluation Whereas in the previous experiment we report results on experimental noisy validation sets matching the optimal decision threshold λ, in this experiment we evaluate our approach in a real inference setting on the shared task training set using a 40-best cosine similarity filter and a fixed λ value of 0.99.

n	found	found (%)	Δ (%)	pairs	Δ (%)
1	6,891	75.84		369,810	
10	7,824	86.11	13.54	3,698,100	900.00
20	8,020	88.27	2.51	7,396,200	100.00
30	8,114	89.30	1.17	11,094,300	50.00
40	8,190	90.14	0.94	14,792,400	33.33
50	8,243	90.72	0.65	18,490,500	25.00
60	8,279	91.12	0.44	22,188,600	20.00
70	8,311	91.47	0.39	25,886,700	16.67
80	8,340	91.79	0.35	29,584,800	14.29
90	8,370	92.12	0.36	33,282,900	12.5
100	8,388	92.32	0.22	36,981,000	11.11
1000	8,752	96.32	4.34	369,810,000	900.00

Table 1: Parallel sentences found from the n-best cosine similarity filter. The Δ columns are the percentage increase in number of parallel sentences found and candidate sentence pairs.

4 Results

4.1 Candidate filtering

In Table 1 we present the information regarding the number of parallel sentences and number of candidate sentence pairs obtained by augmenting the value of n for our candidate filtering method described in 2.2. We see that our cosine similarity filter is able to capture most of the parallel sentence pairs, even for low n values. For $n = 1$, we are surprised to see that such a simple approach using pretrained cross-lingual word embeddings on the Europarl dataset is able to capture 75.84% of the parallel sentence pairs found in the shared task training set. By looking at the Δ columns, we anticipate that there is a precision-recall trade-off by increasing n. For example, if we increase from a 30-best to a 40-best filter, we increase the recall score at most by 0.94%. On the other hand, we augment the number of candidate sentence pairs to evaluate by 33.33%, increasing the risk of false positive examples and a lower precision score. For the shared task we naively used $n = 100$.

4.2 Digits preprocessing

In this experiment we trained two new models on Europarl; by keeping or removing digits. In Table 2 we report the precision, recall and F_1 scores for our three different approaches evaluated on validation sets made of the 9,086 parallel sentences and 50M randomly selected sentences from the shared task training set. The precision-recall curves with respect to different decision threshold values λ are reported in Figure 1. We observe that

---

[4] https://github.com/gouwsmeister/bilbowa

[5] https://comparable.limsi.fr/bucc2017/bucc2017task.html

Model	Precision (%)	Recall (%)	F$_1$ (%)
Digits	83.25	65.86	73.54
Digits to 0	71.41	56.38	63.01
No digits	79.65	63.86	70.89

Table 2: Performance of our models trained on Europarl with three different digits preprocessing method and evaluated on our validation sets made from the shared task training set.

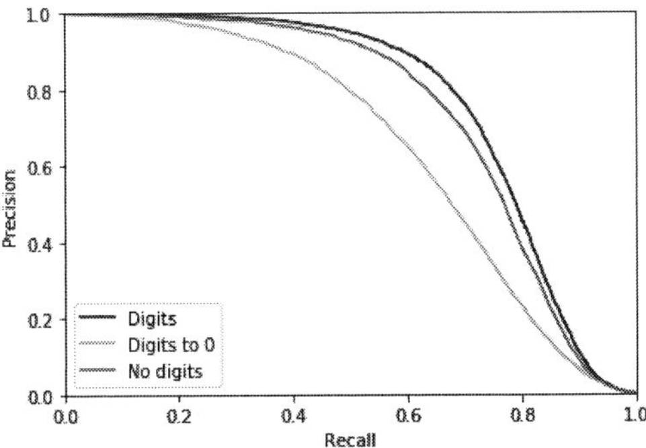

Figure 1: Precision-Recall curve for our models trained on Europarl with three different digits pre-processing method and evaluated on our validation sets made from the shared task training set.

naively replacing the digits to 0, as we did for the shared task, is actually the worst option.

4.3 Model evaluation

Equipped with a filter that seems to work well and a better model trained on a parallel corpus with digits, we expect to obtain a performance in the range of those presented in Section 4.2. Unfortunately for us, it is not the case. Table 3 presents the results we obtained by using our model trained on Europarl with digits, using the 40-best list and $\lambda = 0.99$. One may wonder what happened to our surprisingly low precision score. The problem arises from a combination of how the model is trained on negative examples and how we filtered our candidate sentence pairs. Since our model outputs a positive instance for two sentences sharing an high level of semantic similarity, by filtering the 40 nearest target sentences for each source sentence, we created a pool of candidate sentence pairs that our model outputted as positive most of the time. That being said, those sentence pairs still exist in the Cartesian product of the training set. Thus, the proposed training procedure adding neg-

Decision Threshold	Precision (%)	Recall (%)	F$_1$ (%)
0.99	12.10	70.95	20.67

Table 3: Performance of our models trained on Europarl with digits using the 40-best cosine similarity filter.

ative examples randomly selected from the training set is definitely not adequate and needs to be replaced by a more effective procedure. For future work, instead of random sampling, we propose to apply the n-best cosine similarity filter on our model's training set in a way to select negative examples from the n-best list to train it. A post-processing step could also be useful.

5 Discussion

The idea toward an end-to-end sentence driven approach using deep neural networks for parallel sentence identification is compelling. However, there is much room for improvement. We presented that our initial approach learned on distributional semantics alone has weak points that need to be addressed. With its current architecture and setting, the main issue is the low precision score due to the large amount of false positive examples our system outputs, acting more as a quasi-parallel sentences extractor. The source of this issue comes from the random sampling procedure used to add negative examples to the training set. We have seen that even for a low value n, our simple distributional bag-of-words n-best filter is capable of capturing most parallel sentences found in the comparable corpora, leading to a potentially good recall score. A promising next step would be to use the same n-best filter on our training set and to select negative examples from the n-best list to train our model. We anticipate that selecting negative examples that are similar to the source sentence will allow our approach to capture finer semantic granularities and to have a better precision score. Furthermore, a model trained on negative examples of higher quality should allow us to use a lower optimal decision threshold λ, which increases the recall score.

References

Martin Abadi, Paul Barham, Jianmin Chen, Zhifeng Chen, Andy Davis, Jeffrey Dean, Matthieu Devin,

Sanjay Ghemawat, Geoffrey Irving, Michael Isard, Manjunath Kudlur, Josh Levenberg, Rajat Monga, Sherry Moore, Derek G. Murray, Benoit Steiner, Paul Tucker, Vijay Vasudevan, Pete Warden, Martin Wicke, Yuan Yu, and Xiaoqiang Zheng. 2016. Tensorflow: A system for large-scale machine learning. In *12th USENIX Symposium on Operating Systems Design and Implementation (OSDI 16)*. pages 265–283.

Sadaf Abdul-Rauf and Holger Schwenk. 2009. On the use of comparable corpora to improve smt performance. In *Proceedings of the 12th Conference of the European Chapter of the Association for Computational Linguistics*. Association for Computational Linguistics, Stroudsburg, PA, USA, EACL '09, pages 16–23. http://dl.acm.org/citation.cfm?id=1609067.1609068.

Yoshua Bengio, Rjean Ducharme, Pascal Vincent, and Christian Jauvin. 2003. A neural probabilistic language model. *JOURNAL OF MACHINE LEARNING RESEARCH* 3:1137–1155.

Kyunghyun Cho, Bart van Merrienboer, Caglar Gulcehre, Dzmitry Bahdanau, Fethi Bougares, Holger Schwenk, and Yoshua Bengio. 2014. Learning phrase representations using rnn encoder–decoder for statistical machine translation. In *Proceedings of the 2014 Conference on Empirical Methods in Natural Language Processing (EMNLP)*. Association for Computational Linguistics, Doha, Qatar, pages 1724–1734.

Ronan Collobert and Jason Weston. 2008. A unified architecture for natural language processing: Deep neural networks with multitask learning. In *Proceedings of the 25th International Conference on Machine Learning*. ACM, New York, NY, USA, ICML '08, pages 160–167. https://doi.org/10.1145/1390156.1390177.

Jérémy Ferrero, Frédéric Agnès, Laurent Besacier, and Didier Schwab. 2017. Using word embedding for cross-language plagiarism detection. *CoRR* abs/1702.03082. http://arxiv.org/abs/1702.03082.

Stephan Gouws, Yoshua Bengio, and Greg Corrado. 2015. Bilbowa: Fast bilingual distributed representations without word alignments. In *Proceedings of the 32Nd International Conference on International Conference on Machine Learning - Volume 37*. JMLR.org, ICML'15, pages 748–756.

Alex Graves. 2013. Generating sequences with recurrent neural networks. *CoRR* abs/1308.0850. http://arxiv.org/abs/1308.0850.

Diederik P. Kingma and Jimmy Ba. 2014. Adam: A method for stochastic optimization. *CoRR* abs/1412.6980. http://arxiv.org/abs/1412.6980.

Dragos Stefan Munteanu and Daniel Marcu. 2005. Improving machine translation performance by exploiting non-parallel corpora. *Comput. Linguist.* 31(4):477–504. https://doi.org/10.1162/089120105775299168.

Philip Resnik and Noah A. Smith. 2003. The web as a parallel corpus. *Comput. Linguist.* 29(3):349–380. https://doi.org/10.1162/089120103322711578.

Ilya Sutskever, Oriol Vinyals, and Quoc V. Le. 2014. Sequence to sequence learning with neural networks. In *Proceedings of the 27th International Conference on Neural Information Processing Systems*. MIT Press, Cambridge, MA, USA, NIPS'14, pages 3104–3112. http://dl.acm.org/citation.cfm?id=2969033.2969173.

zNLP: Identifying Parallel Sentences
in Chinese-English Comparable Corpora

Zheng Zhang[1,2]
[1]LIMSI, CNRS, Université Paris-Saclay
Orsay, France
`zheng.zhang@limsi.fr`

Pierre Zweigenbaum[1]
[2] LRI, Univ. Paris-Sud, CNRS,
Université Paris-Saclay
Orsay, France
`pz@limsi.fr`

Abstract

This paper describes the zNLP system for the BUCC 2017 shared task. Our system identifies parallel sentence pairs in Chinese-English comparable corpora by translating word-by-word Chinese sentences into English, using the search engine Solr to select near-parallel sentences and then by using an SVM classifier to identify true parallel sentences from the previous results. It obtains an F1-score of 45% (resp. 43%) on the test (training) set.

1 Introduction

Parallel sentences are used in many natural language processing applications, particularly for automatic terminology extraction (Lefever et al., 2009) and statistical machine translation (Koehn, 2005; Callison-Burch et al., 2004). However, such resources are scarce for many language pairs and domains. Comparable corpora are sets of texts in two or more languages that are selected according to similar specifications, but are not translations of each other (Sharoff et al., 2013; Morin et al., 2015). Nevertheless, parallel sentences, i.e., sentence pairs that are good translations of each other, can occur naturally in such corpora. Therefore many approaches have been proposed to spot parallel sentences in comparable corpora (Munteanu et al., 2004; Smith et al., 2010).

Extracting parallel sentences from comparable monolingual corpora is a very challenging task. According to the shared task web page,[1] *The aim of the Building and Using Comparable Corpora (BUCC) 2017 shared task is to quantitatively evaluate competing methods for extracting parallel sentences from comparable monolingual corpora,* so as to give an overview on the state of the art and to identify the best performing approaches. More precisely, *given two sentence-split monolingual corpora, the task is to identify pairs of sentences that are translations of each other.*

The BUCC 2017 shared task on parallel sentence extraction raises the following three main issues. One is the cross-language problem: as one must compare sentences across languages (here English with German, French, Russian, or Chinese), one must find a way to compare sentences in two different languages, for instance by first translating one language into the other. Another issue is sentence similarity: how do we define and calculate sentence similarity? The last issue is the existence of too many possible sentence combinations: theoretically, for each sentence in a source monolingual corpus, every sentence in the target monolingual corpus could be used to generate a source-target sentence pair for subsequent parallel sentence identification, which would create a quadratic number of candidate sentence pairs.

Previous work (Smith et al., 2010; Munteanu and Marcu, 2005) on parallel sentence extraction from comparable corpora has used external clues for this purpose. (Smith et al., 2010) bootstrapped the process with document-level sentence alignment. (Munteanu and Marcu, 2005) leveraged the publication date of newspaper articles to trim down the number of candidate sentence pairs. These selection methods are not suitable for the BUCC 2017 shared task as no meta-information is provided on the documents from which the corpus sentences are extracted. In this context, we test how similar methods fare without any meta-information.

In this paper, we describe the system that we developed for the BUCC 2017 shared task and show that a translating-searching-classifying three-step approach can achieve promising results

---

[1]`https://comparable.limsi.fr/bucc2017/bucc2017-task.html`

Proceedings of the 10th Workshop on Building and Using Comparable Corpora, pages 51–55,
Vancouver, Canada, August 3, 2017. ©2017 Association for Computational Linguistics

for Chinese-English Comparable Corpora.

2 Proposed Method

To address the three problems of the BUCC 2017 shared task, we propose a method which contains three main steps:

1. 'Translating' the monolingual ZH corpus into English.

2. Searching for candidate source-target parallel sentence pairs.

3. Classifying candidate source-target sentence pairs to find parallel sentences.

Note that in our case, the source data is a monolingual English (henceforth EN) corpus and the target data is a monolingual Chinese (henceforth ZH) corpus.

2.1 'Translating' the monolingual ZH corpus into English

To obtain a translated monolingual ZH corpus, a naive approach has been used: we use the Chinese word segmentation tool *jieba* (v0.38)[2] for word segmentation of all the sentences in the monolingual ZH corpus; then we translate these sentences into English word by word with Chinese-English dictionary resources.

The reason for using jieba is that it supports both traditional Chinese and simplified Chinese, which suits our case as the monolingual ZH corpus contains both types of Chinese characters. Besides, jieba has been widely used and could help users obtain good performance in their systems (Shi et al., 2016; Liu et al., 2015; Zhang et al., 2015).

The Chinese-English dictionary resources are *CC-CEDICT*[3], which contains 54,170 traditional Chinese-simplified Chinese-English entries, and the Chinese-English Translation Lexicon Version 3.0 [LDC2002L27] (Huang et al., 2002), which contains 115,128 simplified Chinese-English entries. The merged Chinese-English dictionary contains 196,398 traditional Chinese-English and simplified Chinese-English entries in total. Additionally, for the words not in these two Chinese-English dictionary resources: we keep the original word as its own translation for the words that

only contain ASCII characters, and the *Microsoft Translator Text API*[4] has been used to obtain translations of the rest. If a Chinese word receives more than one translation in this process, we keep all of them in the translated sentence.

Note that each sentence in the monolingual ZH corpus has a unique ID. In the translated monolingual ZH corpus, each translated sentence keeps the same ID as its original sentence.

2.2 Searching for candidate source-target (EN-ZH) parallel sentence pairs

Apache Solr[5] (version 6.5.1) is used as our candidate source-target parallel sentence pairs search engine. Solr is an open-source full-text search engine. To rank documents for a user query, Solr computes the score of each matching document based on the model's algorithm and ranks them on their relative score (Shahi, 2015).

Here, we use the tf.idf retrieval function of Solr and index each sentence in the translated monolingual ZH corpus separately. We search each sentence in the monolingual EN corpus and select the top N results for each to generate candidate source-target parallel sentence pairs. Then we cut off results whose score is below a score threshold.

If N is large or the score threshold is low, there will be too many candidate source-target parallel sentence pairs for the next step. We attempted to decrease the number of candidate source-target parallel sentence pairs without sacrificing too much search engine's performance. In this purpose, we evaluated *success* on the training set: the proportion of the question set for which a correct answer can be found within the top N documents retrieved for each question, depending on (N, score threshold). This evaluation aims to find the best N and score threshold parameters for Solr that will return less candidate source-target parallel sentence pairs but still with a high success at N. We set our requirement to a success of 85%.

2.3 Classifying candidate source-target parallel sentence pairs to find parallel sentences among them

After obtaining candidate source-target parallel sentence pairs from the previous step, we use

[2]https://github.com/fxsjy/jieba
[3]https://cc-cedict.org/wiki/ (downloaded on March 16, 2017)
[4]https://azure.microsoft.com/en-us/services/cognitive-services/translator-text-api/
[5]http://lucene.apache.org/solr/

an SVM (Support Vector Machine) classifier[6] to identify parallel sentence pairs among them. We define the following 4 features, which can be extracted from candidate source-target parallel sentence pairs:

- Source-target sentence length ratio

- Solr rank

- Solr score

- Word overlap number

When calculating the source-target sentence length ratio, issues might be caused by cases where one Chinese word has more than one translation. To avoid this, the target sentence length is counted as the number of Chinese words of the original sentence in the monolingual ZH corpus instead of the translated one. The other three features are extracted by using sentences in the translated monolingual ZH corpus and the monolingual EN corpus.

The candidate source-target parallel sentence pairs generated by using the BUCC 2017 shared task training set serve as training data for the SVM model. More precisely, the training data are the candidate source-target parallel sentence pairs generated by taking all the sentences in the training monolingual EN corpus as queries to the search engine in Step 2 (with the selected N and score threshold parameters). The source-target sentence pairs that exist in the training gold standard have been considered as positive examples, the rest are negative examples.

After training the SVM model, we use this classifier to predict parallel sentences from the candidate source-target parallel sentence pairs generated by using the BUCC 2017 shared task test set.

2.4 Evaluation protocol

We perform three evaluations: two independent evaluations on the training set for Step 2 (Searching for candidate source-target parallel sentence pairs) and Step 3 (Finding parallel sentences in candidate source-target sentence pairs) and one evaluation on the training and test sets for the whole system. The first two evaluations aim to find the best parameters and configurations of their own part. The last one is for investigating the effectiveness and performance of the whole system.

For the evaluation of Step 2, we use all the English sentences of the training data gold standard as the question set. According to the success evaluation result, we select the parameter N that provides the required success of 85%. Then a Solr score threshold is calculated as the highest threshold that maintains the success on top N.

To find the best configuration (kernel, class_weight, C, gamma parameters) of the SVM classifier, we perform a 5-fold cross-validation on the training data. As the training data (as well as the test data) is highly imbalanced (the number of negative examples is around 120 times higher than the number of positive examples), the class_weight parameter, according to the scikit-learn web page, which *sets the parameter C of class i to class_weight[i]*C for the SVM classifier*, plays an important role.

For the whole system evaluation, after obtaining the final predicted source-target parallel sentence pairs, we use precision, recall and F1-score as evaluation measures:

$$P = \frac{TP}{TP + FP}; R = \frac{TP}{TP + FN}; F1 = \frac{2PR}{P + R}$$

where TP stands for the number of source-target sentence pairs that is present in the gold standard, a false positive FP is a pair of sentences that is not present in the gold standard and a false negative FN is a pair of sentences present in the gold standard but absent from systems results. We tested three configurations:

1. The standard three-step method.

2. Setting N to 1 and replacing the classifier (Step 3) with a baseline ranking method based on the Solr score: we select the M sentence pairs with the highest scores, where M is determined according to the prior probability of being a correct sentence pair, estimated on the training data.

3. The intersection of Configuration 1 and of Configuration 2, with M=10,000.

3 Results and discussion

The success obtained for the training data is shown in Figure 1. We note that the success is close to 85% when we retrieve the top 3 target sentences ($N = 3$) for each source sentence of the gold standard. If we increase N by 1, 88,860 more negative examples (the number of monolingual EN

---

[6]We use the SVC implementation of scikit-learn v0.18, http://scikit-learn.org/stable/

sentences in the training corpus) are added to the SVM classifier's training data, but the success improvement is small. We therefore decided not to increase N and set it to 3. Then the maximum Solr score threshold that does not significantly change the success when $N = 3$ is found to be 15.4.

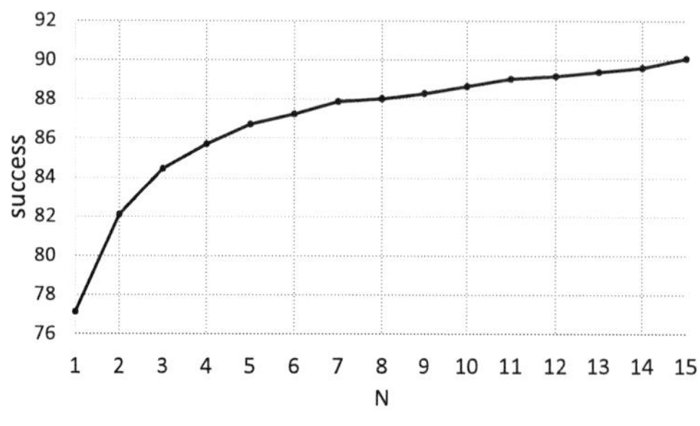

Figure 1: Study of success in the training corpus (evaluation of Step 2)

The results obtained on the training and test sets are presented in Table 1. They are consistent across datasets (test and train): we did not overfit the training set. Our best configuration of SVM classifier for the training data, namely, kernel=rbf, class_weight=1:8, C=1.0, gamma='auto', achieves nearly 0.4037 for precision, 0.4718 for recall and 0.4348 for F1-score. Replacing the classifier with a baseline ranking method only based on the Solr score (Run2) decreases precision, recall and F1-score to 0.2254. This illustrates that only using the tf.idf-based Solr score is not sufficient for the task. Besides, as could be expected, Run 3, the intersection of Runs 1 and 2 is more precise, but incurs a strong decrease in recall. Its recall remains higher than that of Run 2 because it uses a higher M.

Corpus	P	R	F
Training: Run 1	0.4037	**0.4718**	**0.4348**
Training: Run 2	0.2254	0.2254	0.2254
Training: Run 3	**0.4416**	0.4053	0.4227
Test: Run 1	0.4247	**0.4815**	**0.4513**
Test: Run 2	0.2296	0.2300	0.2298
Test: Run 3	**0.4529**	0.4161	0.4338

Table 1: Evaluation results: Run 1 = three steps, Run 2 = no classifier, Run 3 = intersection

We also performed experiments without using the Microsoft Translator Text API. In that case, there is no big change in success. On the test set, with the standard three-step method, this increased recall (0.5153) but decreased precision (0.3158) and F1-score (0.3916).

The whole system does not require external resources other than a Chinese-English dictionary. It is fast: 'translating' the monolingual ZH corpus takes around 1 minute; searching for candidate source-target parallel sentence pairs takes less than 5 minutes for the whole monolingual ZH corpus in the training or test data; the final SVM classifier takes around 20 minutes for training but less than 5 minutes for feature extraction and source-target parallel sentence pairs prediction after obtaining the trained SVM model. However, as the first step's translation is at the word level instead of the sentence level, and for one Chinese word, there are 4.67 English translations on average, we may lose context information of the original words and sentences in the monolingual ZH corpus.

4   Conclusion

In this paper we described the zNLP system for the BUCC 2017 shared task. We proposed a three-step approach to parallel sentence identification in Chinese-English Comparable Corpora by 'translating' the monolingual ZH corpus into English, filtering out candidate parallel sentence pairs with Solr and then selecting the final parallel source-target sentence pairs by using an SVM classifier. Our system identifies parallel sentences with an F1-score of 45.13% in the test data. The proposed method is fast and does not rely on external resources except a Chinese-English dictionary. The code is publicly available at `https://github.com/zzcoolj/Parallel-Sentences-Identifier`.

Potential pathways for future work include adding more filter conditions to Step 2 (e.g sentence length ratio, word overlap threshold) for candidate source-target parallel sentence pairs. Another pathway would be to add more features to the SVM model. Also in our system, we obtain candidate sentence pairs by searching each sentence in the monolingual EN corpus after indexing each sentence in the translated monolingual ZH corpus separately. We plan to do the reverse (searching sentences in the translated monolingual ZH corpus and indexing the monolingual EN corpus) and combine the two results as our new candidate source-target parallel sentence pairs. We also plan to extend our system to other language pairs by using the relevant dictionaries or word-aligned parallel corpora.

References

Chris Callison-Burch, David Talbot, and Miles Osborne. 2004. Statistical machine translation with word-and sentence-aligned parallel corpora. In *Proceedings of the 42nd Annual Meeting on Association for Computational Linguistics*. Association for Computational Linguistics, page 175.

Shudong Huang, David Graff, and George Doddington. 2002. *Multiple-Translation Chinese Corpus [LDC2002T01]*. Linguistic Data Consortium, Philadelphia. Web download file.

Philipp Koehn. 2005. Europarl: A parallel corpus for statistical machine translation. In *MT summit*. Citeseer, volume 5, pages 79–86.

Els Lefever, Lieve Macken, and Veronique Hoste. 2009. Language-independent bilingual terminology extraction from a multilingual parallel corpus. In *Proceedings of the 12th Conference of the European Chapter of the Association for Computational Linguistics*. Association for Computational Linguistics, pages 496–504.

Xuebo Liu, Shuang Ye, Xin Li, Yonghao Luo, and Yanghui Rao. 2015. Zhihurank: A topic-sensitive expert finding algorithm in community question answering websites. In *International Conference on Web-Based Learning*. Springer, pages 165–173.

Emmanuel Morin, Amir Hazem, Florian Boudin, and Elizaveta Loginova Clouet. 2015. LINA: Identifying comparable documents from Wikipedia. In *Eighth Workshop on Building and Using Comparable Corpora*.

Dragos Stefan Munteanu, Alexander M Fraser, and Daniel Marcu. 2004. Improved machine translation performance via parallel sentence extraction from comparable corpora. In *HLT-NAACL*. pages 265–272.

Dragos Stefan Munteanu and Daniel Marcu. 2005. Improving machine translation performance by exploiting non-parallel corpora. *Computational Linguistics* 31(4):477–504.

Dikshant Shahi. 2015. Solr scoring. In *Apache Solr*, Springer, pages 189–207.

Serge Sharoff, Reinhard Rapp, and Pierre Zweigenbaum. 2013. Overviewing important aspects of the last twenty years of research in comparable corpora. In Serge Sharoff, Reinhard Rapp, Pierre Zweigenbaum, and Pascale Fung, editors, *Building and Using Comparable Corpora*, Springer, Berlin Heidelberg, pages 1–20.

Hongjie Shi, Takashi Ushio, Mitsuru Endo, Katsuyoshi Yamagami, and Noriaki Horii. 2016. A multichannel convolutional neural network for cross-language dialog state tracking. In *Spoken Language Technology Workshop (SLT), 2016 IEEE*. IEEE, pages 559–564.

Jason R Smith, Chris Quirk, and Kristina Toutanova. 2010. Extracting parallel sentences from comparable corpora using document level alignment. In *Human Language Technologies: The 2010 Annual Conference of the North American Chapter of the Association for Computational Linguistics*. Association for Computational Linguistics, pages 403–411.

Xiang Zhang, Junbo Zhao, and Yann LeCun. 2015. Character-level convolutional networks for text classification. In *Advances in neural information processing systems*. pages 649–657.

BUCC2017: A Hybrid Approach for Identifying Parallel Sentences in Comparable Corpora

Sainik Kumar Mahata[1]
sainik.mahata@gmail.com

Dipankar Das[2]
ddas@cse.jdvu.ac.in

Sivaji Bandyopadhyay[3]
sbandyopadhyay@cse.jdvu.ac.in

[1,2,3] Department of Computer Science and Engineering, Jadavpur University, India

Abstract

A Statistical Machine Translation (SMT) system is always trained using large parallel corpus to produce effective translation. Not only is the corpus scarce, it also involves a lot of manual labor and cost. Parallel corpus can be prepared by employing comparable corpora where a pair of corpora is in two different languages pointing to the same domain. In the present work, we try to build a parallel corpus for French-English language pair from a given comparable corpus. The data and the problem set are provided as part of the shared task organized by BUCC 2017. We have proposed a system that first translates the sentences by heavily relying on Moses and then group the sentences based on sentence length similarity. Finally, the one to one sentence selection was done based on Cosine Similarity algorithm.

1 Introduction

Statistical Machine Translation (SMT) analyzes the output of human translators using statistical methods and extracts information about the translation process from corpora of translated texts. SMT has shown good results for many language pairs and is responsible for the recent surge in terms of popularity of Machine Translation among the research communities. But, for a SMT system to work efficiently, it has to be fed with large parallel corpus, for producing high quality phrase table and translation models (Brown et. al., 1991; Church et. al., 1993; Dagan et. al., 1999). Since availability of large parallel corpus is an issue for low resourced languages, building one from scratch involves high manual labor and cost (Pal et. al., 2014; Tan and Pal, 2014; Mahata et. al., 2016). This is the reason why lot of research has gone into the concept of building parallel corpus, from comparable corpus (Jagarla-

mudi et. al., 2011; Kay and Roscheisen, 1993; Kupiec, 1993; Lardilleux et. al., 2012). A comparable corpus is a pair of monolingual corpus in the same domain, where the sentences in the both the corpus are not aligned. The proposed work deals with identifying parallel sentences from such a comparable corpus provided by BUCC 2017[1] shared task. Sample, training and test data contain monolingual corpora split into sentences, in the format, *"utf-8 text, with UNIX end-of-lines; identifiers are made of a two-letter language code + 9 digits, separated by a dash '- '"*:

- Monolingual EN corpus (where EN stands for English), one tab-separated sentence_id + sentence per line.
- Monolingual FR corpus (where FR stands for Foreign, e.g. French), one tab-separated sentence_id + sentence per line.
- Gold standard list of tab-separated EN-FR sentence_id pairs (held out for the test data)

The algorithm of the proposed work has been constructed primarily using Moses (Koehn, 2015) toolkit that has been fed with parallel corpus from Europarl[2], with French as the source language and English as the target language. Also, the similarity based on sentence length has been used for the preliminary alignment because equivalent sentences in comparable corpus may roughly correspond with respect to length. Cosine Similarity algorithm was used for the final alignment. Section 2 will discuss the proposed algorithm in detail and will be followed by results and discussions in Section 3 and Section 4, respectively.

---

1 https://comparable.limsi.fr/bucc2017/bucc2017-task.html
2 http://www.statmt.org/europarl/

Proceedings of the 10th Workshop on Building and Using Comparable Corpora, pages 56–59,
Vancouver, Canada, August 3, 2017. ©2017 Association for Computational Linguistics

```
Le pays est un carrefour de l'Asie qui voit passer de nombreux peuples par son territoire.  The country is a crossroads of Asia which sees
many peoples pass through its territory.
Cette région est cependant le noyau de vastes empires comme l'Empire bactrien, l'Empire kouchan ou encore l'Empire ghaznévide.  This region,
however, is the nucleus of vast empires such as the Bactrian Empire, the Kushan Empire or the Empire Ghazn Empire.
Le pays devient ainsi un État tampon de 1879 à 1919, demeurant indépendant sur le plan de la politique intérieure.  The country thus becomes
a buffer state from 1879 to 1919, remaining independent on the domestic policy level.
En 1996 un gouvernement islamiste, celui des talibans, prend le pouvoir et est chassé par une coalition internationale en 2001.  In 1996, an
Islamist government, the Taliban government, took power and was expelled by an international coalition in 2001.
L'Afghanistan est un pays montagneux avec des plaines au Nord et au Sud-Ouest.  Afghanistan is a mountainous country with plains to the north
and southwest.
De grandes parties du pays sont arides, et l'eau fraîche est limitée.  Large parts of the country are arid, and fresh water is limited.
```

Figure 1: Translation of French sentences into English sentences using Moses.

```
fr-000000001    The country is a crossroads of Asia which sees many peoples pass through its territory.
fr-000000002    This region, however, is the nucleus of vast empires such as the Bactrian Empire, the Kushan Empire or the Empire Ghazn
Empire.
fr-000000003    The country thus becomes a buffer state from 1879 to 1919, remaining independent on the domestic policy level.
fr-000000004    In 1996, an Islamist government, the Taliban government, took power and was expelled by an international coalition in
2001.
fr-000000005    Afghanistan is a mountainous country with plains to the north and southwest.
fr-000000006    Large parts of the country are arid, and fresh water is limited.
```

Figure 2: Appending sentence_id's to translated English sentence

2   Proposed System

2.1   Building baseline Statistical Machine Translation Model

Moses is a statistical machine translation system that allows you to automatically train translation models for any language pair, when trained with a large collection of translated texts (parallel corpus). Once the model has been trained, an efficient search algorithm quickly finds the highest probability translation among the exponential number of choices. For the given system, Moses was trained with French (Fr) as the source language and English (En) as the target language. The En-Fr parallel corpus that was used to train Moses has been downloaded from Europarl Corpus. The language model training of Moses was done by concatenating the English corpus of Europarl and the English text of the test data provided by BUCC 2017. The French corpora from the given test data was taken and sentences were extracted barring the sentence_id's. The extracted French sentences were then fed to Moses to get translated English sentences as output. Example of this process is shown in Figure 1. The segregated sentence_id's from the previous step were again appended to the translated English sentences. Example of this process is shown in Figure 2.

2.2   Sentence similarity based on sentence length

Gale and Church (1991) in their paper, proposed a system for aligning corresponding sentences in a parallel corpora, based on the principle that equivalent sentences should roughly correspond in length—that is, longer sentences in one language should correspond to longer sentences in

the other language. This idea forms the basis of our preliminary alignment system, which tries to align sentence pairs based on their length. We have found out the length of the translated English sentence and have found matches in the sentences of the English text from the test data. This results in one-to-many relationship between the translated English and the English sentences from the test data. The variance in this step is kept as 4, which means if the length of the English sentences of the test data exceeds or falls behind by a factor of 4, when compared to the translated English sentence, they are also included in this step. This is done for reducing the time complexity of the Cosine Similarity search algorithm. Example of this step is shown in Figure 4.

2.3   Final alignment using Cosine Similarity Algorithm

Cosine similarity is particularly used in positive space, where the outcome is neatly bounded in [0, 1]. The formula used in our approach is as follows.

$$Similarity = \cos(\theta) = \frac{A.B}{\|A\|\|B\|} = \frac{\sum_{i=1}^{n} A_i B_i}{\sqrt{\sum_{i=1}^{n} A_i^2} \sqrt{\sum_{i=1}^{n} B_i^2}}$$

$$(1)$$

Where "A" and "B" are the translated English sentence and one of the English sentences from the test data found out using the preliminary alignment system, respectively. One sentence from the translated English corpus is taken and is matched with the selected sentences in English corpus from the test data, using the Cosine Similarity algorithm.

The sentence pair with the highest Cosine Similarity value is considered as the final alignment. Sentence_id's of the selected sentence pair are extracted and given as output. An example of the output format is shown in Figure 3.

```
fr-000000001    en-000121474
fr-000000002    en-000313524
fr-000000003    en-000292858
fr-000000004    en-000043944
fr-000000005    en-000193935
fr-000000006    en-000210237
fr-000000007    en-000269236
fr-000000008    en-000193986
fr-000000009    en-000218701
fr-000000010    en-000315531
```

Figure 3: Final alignment using Cosine Similarity

```
en-000000001    Like all "Guild Wars" campaigns, "Prophecies" contains a co-operative role-playing portion and a competitive Player versus
Player (PvP) portion.
fr-000000004    In 1996, an Islamist government, the Taliban government, took power and was expelled by an international coalition in 2001.
fr-000000014    The Afghans consider the medieval name of their country is Khorassan which currently designates a region of northeastern
Iran.
fr-000000029    The founder of Afghanistan also bears the title of "Bábé Málà", which, in pachto, means father of the Nation.
fr-000000034    Having left no instructions or protocol on his succession, Ahmad Shâh had complicated the succession to the Afghan throne.
fr-000000035    For the leaders of the time, it was no secret that Timour Shâh had the preference of his father.
fr-000000039    The young Timur was able to enter the city of Kandahar and be crowned Padishah of the Afghan Empire.
fr-000000048    The sudden death of Timur Shah Durrani opens an era of war and tears for succession to the throne.
fr-000000064    The Soviet Union unilaterally decided to leave the country in February 1989, leaving Nadjibullah in control of the country.
fr-000000070    Members of Hezb-Â © -islami (party of Hekmatyar) enter the government of President Rabbani while Hekmatyar becomes prime
minister.
fr-000000087    Afghanistan will receive about 400 million euros in royalties per year for 30 years, the duration of the concession.
fr-000000089    Its vineyards are so abundant that the grains are given, for three months of the year, to the cattle.
fr-000000105    The exploitation of iron ores is not currently on the agenda, but represents a huge potential for the country.
```

Figure 4: Finding corresponding sentences with respect to Gale and Church algorithm.

```
fr-000000005    en-000193935    L'Afghanistan est un pays montagneux avec des plaines au Nord et au Sud-Ouest.  A landlocked mountainous
country with plains in the north and southwest, Afghanistan is located within South Asia and Central Asia. 1  3
fr-000000007    en-000269236    L'Afghanistan a un climat continental, avec des étés chauds et des hivers froids.  Ruse has a continental
climate () with very hot summers and relatively cold winters.    1  3
fr-000000079    en-000222220    La guerre d'Afghanistan est particulièrement liée au conflit armé du Nord-Ouest du Pakistan.    The
conflict in Afghanistan also forced millions of Afghan refugees into Pakistan, particularly in the northwestern regions.    1  2
fr-000000134    en-000251190    Il existe 40 langues répertoriées en Afghanistan dont 2 langues officielles nationales, le dari et le
pachto.  Pashto and Dari are both designated as the official languages of Afghanistan.    1  3
fr-000000138    en-000315065    L'Afrique du Sud est aussi la première puissance politique et militaire en Afrique. South Africa is the
largest economic and military power in the SADC.    1  4
fr-000000213    en-000087663    Le taux de violence sexuelle en Afrique du Sud était, en 2000, le plus élevé au monde.  The rate of sexual
violence in South Africa is among the highest in the world. 1  4
```

Figure 5: Result of evaluation.

3   Evaluation

BUCC 2017 provided us with an evaluation script and a gold standard data to calculate the Precision, Recall and F-Score. This is shown in Figure 5. The calculation was done using value TP, FP and FN, where TP (true positive) is a pair of sentences that is present in the gold standard, FP (false positive) is a pair of sentences that is not present in the gold standard and FN (false negative) is a pair of sentences present in the gold standard but absent from system. We submitted 38,736 sentence pair alignment. Table 1 shows the results.

Proposed System	
TP	10111 pairs
FP	37725 pairs
FN	8032 pairs
Precision	0.0261
Recall	0.1118
F-Score	0.0423

Table 1: Evaluation Results.

4   Discussion

We tested the proposed approach by training Moses for translating English to French as well. The English data from the test data corpus was translated to Spanish. After preliminary alignment, Cosine Similarity was sought for translated Spanish and Spanish corpus of the test data. After testing the system with the gold standard, we found out only one match.

Second Evaluation	
TP	3 pairs
FP	20779 pairs
FN	9040 pairs
Precision	0.0001
Recall	0.0003
F-Score	0.0002

Table 2: Second evaluation Results.

As a future prospect, we would like to align the sentences based on Named-Entity and Edit distance approach.

5 Conclusion

The paper proposes a Hybrid approach for sentence alignment in comparable corpora. Moses toolkit was used for building the baseline translation system along with similarity based on sentence length and Cosine Similarity algorithms. The evaluation of the proposed method yielded results as Precision: 0.0261 Recall: 0.1118 and F-Score: 0.0423.

References

Peter F. Brown, Jennifer C. Lai, and Robert L. Mercer. 1991. Aligning sentences in parallel corpora. In Proceedings of the 29th Annual Meeting on Association for Computational Linguistics, ACL '91, pages 169–176, Stroudsburg, PA, USA. Association for Computational Linguistics.

Kenneth Ward Church. 1993. Char align: A program for aligning parallel texts at the character level. In Proceedings of the 31st Annual Conference of the Association for Computational Linguistics, pages 1–8.

I. Dagan, K. Church, and W. Gale, 1999. Natural Language Processing Using Very Large Corpora, chapter Robust Bilingual Word Alignment for Machine Aided Translation, pages 209–224. Springer Netherlands, Dordrecht.

William A. Gale and Kenneth W. Church. 1991. A program for aligning sentences in bilingual corpora. In Proceedings of the 29th Annual Meeting on Association for Computational Linguistics, ACL '91, pages 177–184, Stroudsburg, PA, USA. Association for Computational Linguistics.

Jagadeesh Jagarlamudi, Hal Daume, III, and Raghavendra Udupa. 2011. From bilingual dictionaries to interlingua document representations. In Proceedings of the 49th Annual Meeting of the Association for Computational Linguistics: Human Language Technologies: Short Papers - Volume2, HLT '11, pages 147–152, Stroudsburg, PA,USA. Association for Computational Linguistics.

Martin Kay and Martin Roscheisen. 1993. Text- translation alignment. Comput. Linguist.,19(1):121–142, March.

Julian Kupiec. 1993. An algorithm for finding noun phrase correspondences in bilingual corpora. In Proceedings of the 31st Annual Meeting on Association for Computational Linguistics, ACL '93,pages 17–22, Stroudsburg, PA, USA. Association for Computational Linguistics.

Adrien Lardilleux, Franois Yvon, and Yves Lepage.2012. Hierarchical sub-sentential alignment with Anymalign. pages 279–286, Trento, Italy.

Yuji Matsumoto, Hiroyuki Ishimoto, and Takehito Utsuro.1993. Structural matching of parallel texts. In Proceedings of the 31st Annual Meeting on Association for Computational Linguistics, ACL '93,pages 23–30, Stroudsburg, PA, USA. Association for Computational Linguistics.

Santanu Pal, Partha Pakray, and Sudip Kumar Naskar.2014. Automatic building and using parallel resources for smt from comparable corpora. Proceedings of the 3rd Workshop on Hybrid Approaches to Translation (HyTra) @ EACL, pages 48–57.

Alexandre Patry and Philippe Langlais, 2005. Automatic Identification of Parallel Documents With Light or Without Linguistic Resources, pages 354–365. Springer Berlin Heidelberg, Berlin, Heidelberg.

Michel Simard, George F. Foster, and Pierre Isabelle.1992. Using cognates to align sentences in bilingual corpora. In in Proceedings of the Fourth International Conference on Theoretical and Methodological Issues in Machine Translation, pages 67–81.

Liling Tan and Santanu Pal. 2014. Manawi: Using multi-word expressions and named entities to improve machine translation. Proceedings of the Ninth Workshop on Statistical Machine Translation, pages201–206.

Thuy Vu, Ai Ti Aw, and Min Zhang. 2009. Feature based method for document alignment in comparable news corpora. In Proceedings of the 12thConerence of the European Chapter of the Association for Computational Linguistics, EACL '09,pages 843–851, Stroudsburg, PA, USA. Association for Computational Linguistics.

Philipp Koehn, Hieu Hoang, Alexandra Birch, Chris Callison-Burch, Marcello Federico, Nicola Bertoldi, Brooke Cowan, Wade Shen, Christine Moran, Richard Zens, Chris Dyer, Ondrej Bojar, Alexandra Constantin, Evan Herbst, Moses: Open Source Toolkit for Statistical Machine Translation, Annual Meeting of the Association for Computational Linguistics (ACL), demonstration session, Prague, Czech Republic, June 2007.

Sainik Kumar Mahata, Dipankar Das, and Santanu Pal. 2016. WMT2016: A Hybrid Approach to Bilingual Document Alignment. In proceedings of the First Conference on Machine Translation, Volume 2: Shared Task Papers, pages 724–727, Berlin, Germany, August 11-12, 2016.

Overview of the Second BUCC Shared Task:
Spotting Parallel Sentences in Comparable Corpora

Pierre Zweigenbaum
LIMSI, CNRS,
Université Paris-Saclay,
F-91405 Orsay, France
`pz@limsi.fr`

Serge Sharoff
University of Leeds,
Leeds, United Kingdom
`s.sharoff@leeds.ac.uk`

Reinhard Rapp
Magdeburg-Stendal University
of Applied Sciences and
University of Mainz, Germany
`reinhardrapp@gmx.de`

Abstract

This paper presents the BUCC 2017 shared task on parallel sentence extraction from comparable corpora. It recalls the design of the datasets, presents their final construction and statistics and the methods used to evaluate system results. 13 runs were submitted to the shared task by 4 teams, covering three of the four proposed language pairs: French-English (7 runs), German-English (3 runs), and Chinese-English (3 runs). The best F-scores as measured against the gold standard were 0.84 (German-English), 0.80 (French-English), and 0.43 (Chinese-English). Because of the design of the dataset, in which not all gold parallel sentence pairs are known, these are only minimum values. We examined manually a small sample of the false negative sentence pairs for the most precise French-English runs and estimated the number of parallel sentence pairs not yet in the provided gold standard. Adding them to the gold standard leads to revised estimates for the French-English F-scores of at most +1.5pt. This suggests that the BUCC 2017 datasets provide a reasonable approximate evaluation of the parallel sentence spotting task.

1 Introduction

Shared tasks and the associated datasets have proved their worth as a driving force in a number of subfields of Natural Language Processing. However, very few shared tasks were organized on the topic of comparable corpora. Therefore, we endeavored to design and organize shared tasks as companions of the BUCC workshop se-

ries on Building and Using Comparable Corpora. The First BUCC Shared Task (Sharoff et al., 2015) tackled the detection of comparable documents across languages. The Second BUCC Shared Task,[1] presented here, addresses the detection of parallel sentences across languages in non-aligned, monolingual corpora.

Let us recall the overall goals, design and principles of this task, which were introduced in (Zweigenbaum et al., 2016). A bottleneck in statistical machine translation is the scarceness of parallel resources for many language pairs and domains. Previous research has shown that this bottleneck can be reduced by utilizing parallel portions found within comparable corpora (Utiyama and Isahara, 2003; Munteanu et al., 2004; Abdul-Rauf and Schwenk, 2009). These are useful for many purposes, including automatic terminology extraction and the training of statistical MT systems. However, past work relied on meta-information, such as the publication date of news articles or inter-language links in Wikipedia documents, to help select promising sentence pairs before examining them more thoroughly. It is therefore difficult to separate the heuristic part of the methods that deals with this meta-information in clever ways from the cross-language part of the methods that deals with translation and comparability issues. We consider that the latter type of methods is more fundamental and wanted to focus on its evaluation. We thus designed a task in which no meta-information is available on the relation between the two monolingual corpora in which pairs of translated sentences are to be found.

In (Zweigenbaum et al., 2016) we showed the difference of this task to PAN's cross-language plagiarism detection (Potthast et al., 2012), SemEval's cross-language semantic text similarity

---

[1] `https://comparable.limsi.fr/bucc2017/`
`bucc2017-task.html`

Proceedings of the 10th Workshop on Building and Using Comparable Corpora, pages 60–67,
Vancouver, Canada, August 3, 2017. ©2017 Association for Computational Linguistics

(Agirre et al., 2016), and WMT's bilingual document alignment (Buck and Koehn, 2016).

The present paper reports the actual organization of the task as a companion to the BUCC 2017 workshop. We describe the final method we used to prepare bilingual corpora in four language pairs: Chinese-English, French-English, German-English, and Russian-English (Section 2), the evaluation method (Section 3), the participants' systems (Section 4), the results they obtained (Section 5), and conclude (Section 6).

2 Corpus preparation

The challenges we faced to prepare corpora for a parallel sentence spotting shared task, and the measures we took to address them, were the following.

1. Given two monolingual corpora, it would be very long for human evaluators to find all sentence pairs that are translations of each other. Therefore we decided to insert known parallel sentence pairs into existing monolingual corpora. We chose Wikipedia articles (20161201 dumps [2]) as our monolingual corpora and News Commentary (v11[3]) as our source for parallel sentence pairs. In the remainder of this section we use French and English as a running example of a language pair.

2. These inserted parallel sentence pairs should not be trivially detectable in the monolingual corpora. Therefore we strove to insert sentences that are coherent with the context in which they are inserted. In this purpose we aimed to select as insertion points sentences that were similar in topic to the inserted sentences. We implemented this by indexing with the Solr search engine each English sentence of the monolingual corpus (English Wikipedia dump, converted to text and split into sentences) and each French sentence of the monolingual corpus (French Wikipedia dump, converted to text and split into sentences). For each sentence pair in the parallel corpus (French-English News Commentary), we queried Solr to find the most similar French sentence and English sentence for this pair; if hits were found for both languages, we recorded as insertion point for the French parallel sentence the French sentence found, and as insertion point for the English parallel sentence the English sentence found. We performed the actual insertion after all parallel sentence pairs were thus processed.

Additionally, a different distribution of sentence lengths in the original monolingual sentences and in the inserted sentences might give hints about the origin of a sentence. Therefore we aimed at having similar distributions of sentence lengths for both the Wikipedia sentences and the News Commentary sentences. In this purpose, we excluded sentences outside a range of lengths (we kept sentences between 20 and 40 words long).

We also tried to reduce trivial typographical differences that may be revealing of the source of a sentence, such as the use of certain quotation marks and certain systematic conversion issues found in Wikipedia texts after conversion from their Wiki source. In this purpose we customized an existing Wikipedia conversion tool, WikiExtractor.py,[4] to include sentence splitting (with NLTK). Since template processing was the cause of a large number of idiosyncrasies in the converted Wikipedia text, we removed the sentences that contained a template.

3. The original monolingual texts should contain as few 'natural' parallel sentence pairs as possible. Since interlinked Wikipedia articles are a common source of parallel sentence pairs, we ensured that a given dataset never contained sentences from such a pair of documents.

4. When the two sentences in a parallel pair are inserted in the monolingual corpora, there is no particular reason for them to be positioned in similar locations in the two corpora. Therefore, once a corpus has been generated this way, splitting it into training and test would be likely to separate a number of parallel pairs. Besides, an additional small *sample* split was also needed for prospective participants to examine data and decide whether they would be interested, extending the problem further.

To prevent this problem, we split each pair of monolingual corpora, before indexing and parallel sentence insertion, into sample, training and test corpus pairs, respectively with 2%, 49% and 49% of the full corpora (the number and sizes of these splits are specified as parameters to the algorithm). Given as input two sets of Wikipedia pages, the algorithm randomly distributes them into the N splits according to the specified probabilities. It

[2]http://ftp.acc.umu.se/mirror/
wikimedia.org/dumps/
[3]http://www.casmacat.eu/corpus/
news-commentary.html
[4]https://github.com/attardi/
wikiextractor

Pair	Sample (2%)			Training (49%)			Test (49%)		
	fr	en	gold	*fr*	en	gold	*fr*	en	gold
de-en	32593	40354	1038	413869	399337	9580	413884	396534	9550
fr-en	21497	38069	929	271874	369810	9086	276833	373459	9043
ru-en	45459	72766	2374	460853	558401	14435	457327	566356	14330
zh-en	8624	13589	257	94637	88860	1899	91824	90037	1896

Table 1: Corpus statistics: number of monolingual sentences (*fr*, en) and of parallel pairs (gold) for each split and each language pair. The *fr* column stands for the non-English language in each pair.

Name	Affiliation	Language pairs
VIC	Vicomtech-IK4, Donostia / San Sebastian, Gipuzkoa, Spain	de-en (3), fr-en (3)
RALI	RALI - DIRO, Université de Montréal, Montréal, Québec, Canada	fr-en (3)
JUNLP	Department of Computer Science and Engineering, Jadavpur University, India	fr-en (1)
zNLP	LIMSI, CNRS, Université Paris-Saclay, Orsay, France	zh-en (3)

Table 2: Shared task systems

also ensures that no interlinked pair of pages is distributed to the same split. Indexing, searching and sentence insertion were then performed on each split separately. Since the training and test sets for a given language pair were generated with the same process and parameters, they received very similar numbers of parallel sentence pairs.

This process was applied to five languages (Chinese (zh), English (en), French (fr), German (de), Russian (ru)) to produce four bilingual datasets, each split into sample, training, and test data. Table 1 shows the statistics of the resulting datasets.

3 Evaluation method

Given two sentence-split monolingual corpora, participant systems were expected to identify pairs of sentences that are translations of each other. Each team was allowed to submit up to three runs per language pair.

Evaluation was performed using balanced F-score. In the results of a system, a true positive TP is a pair of sentences that is present in the gold standard and a false positive FP is a pair of sentences that is not present in the gold standard. A false negative FN is a pair of sentences present in the gold standard but absent from system results. Precision, Recall and F1-score were then computed using the usual formulas.

Of note, this evaluation is performed on the synthetic corpus presented above, using the inserted parallel sentence pairs as the gold standard. Therefore it does not take into account the possible existence of true parallel pairs present in the monolingual corpora beyond the inserted sentence pairs. By avoiding aligned Wikipedia articles, the construction of the corpus attempted to reduce the likelihood of such sentence pairs, but indeed it did not suppress it altogether. For these reasons we also performed a limited experiment in which human judges evaluated selected samples of the system results. The assessment of each sentence pair was performed according to the guidelines of the SemEval 2016 cross-language sentence similarity task (Agirre et al., 2016).

4 Participants and systems

About 17 teams downloaded datasets, among which four teams submitted runs: VIC (Spain) (Azpeitia et al., 2017), RALI (Canada) (Grégoire and Langlais, 2017), JUNLP (India) (Mahata et al., 2017), and LIMSI (France: 'zNLP') (Zhang and Zweigenbaum, 2017). Table 2 gives more detail about teams and runs.

All systems had to include a way to cope with the bilingual dimension of the task. This was addressed with pre-existing dictionaries (LIMSI), machine translation systems (JUNLP, LIMSI), word alignments obtained from parallel corpora (VIC), or bilingual word embeddings trained from parallel corpora (RALI).

Cross-language sentence similarity was then handled by Cosine similarity (JUNLP, LIMSI, RALI) or the Jaccard coefficient (VIC), possibly with weighting (a function of frequency: VIC; tf.idf: LIMSI) and with a trained classifier (RALI, LIMSI). Some teams used an Information Retrieval engine to accelerate the search for similar sentences (VIC, LIMSI).

JUNLP (Mahata et al., 2017) implemented a baseline method that translates the FR corpus with a Machine Translation system, selects candidate sentence pairs with a suitable length ratio, and chooses the final sentence pairs based on Cosine similarity.

zNLP (Zhang and Zweigenbaum, 2017) used a bilingual dictionary to perform word-level translation of the ZH corpus, complemented by calls to an on-line Machine Translation system. They used the Solr search engine to index sentences and search for similar sentences, collecting a number of candidate translations for each 'source' sentence. They selected the best translation (or none) by training a classifier with Solr score and rank, word overlap, and sentence length features.

RALI (Grégoire and Langlais, 2017) experimented with a deep learning framework. They trained bilingual word embeddings with Bil-BOWA (Bilingual Bag-of-Words without Alignments (Gouws et al., 2015)) on the Europarl parallel corpus, represented source and target sentences in this common space and used Cosine similarity to select candidate parallel sentence pairs. They also trained a bidirectional recurrent neural network with gated recurrent units (BiGRU) on both the source and target languages to build sentence-level continuous representations. They learned a linear transformation of these representations from one language to the other and decided on the parallelism of two sentences based on the comparison of their continuous representations through this transformation.

VIC (Azpeitia et al., 2017) used probabilistic dictionaries acquired by word alignment of parallel corpora to translate each corpus. They used the Lucune search engine to index sentences and search for similar sentences, collecting a number of candidate translations for each 'source' sentence, in both directions. Final sentence similarity is computed by their STACC method (Set-Theoretic Alignment for Comparable Corpora, (Etchegoyhen and Azpeitia, 2016)), which extends basic word overlap by taking into account non-matched words that share a long enough common prefix, as well as numbers and capitalized true-cased tokens. STACC measures word overlap with the Jaccard coefficient. They refined the STACC method by taking into account lexical weights that penalize frequent words.

5 Results and discussion

We first present an evaluation based upon the inserted translation pairs (Section 5.1) then an additional evaluation based upon human judgment of sample system results (Section 5.2)

5.1 Automatic evaluation

We present here the evaluation results for the submitted runs for each language in turn. As explained above, these results are based on the artificially inserted translation pairs. In each table we show the precision, recall and F1-score of each run in percentages. Because this synthetic dataset represents an approximation of a real task, there is no point in computing precise scores: we round the computed percentages to the nearest integer.

Additionally, we observed that some participants took into account the prior probability of translation pairs in the training datasets. Given that the test dataset was announced to be generated in the same way as the training dataset, they targeted a number of translation pairs in the test that was consistent with this prior probability. We therefore display this number of translation pairs in the tables too.

Three teams submitted runs on the French-English (fr-en) language pair. In addition to these runs, Table 3 presents the minimum, maximum, median, mean and standard deviation for each measure. The initial JUNLP submission had a bug which was fixed a couple of days later; we show the results of the fixed submission in italics, but did not include it in the additional statistics. The VIC results confirm the strategy described in

run_name	sys_n	P (%)	R (%)	F1 (%)
VIC1	8831	80	79	**79**
VIC2	7569	**87**	73	**79**
VIC3	10768	70	**83**	76
RALI2	47576	12	63	20
RALI1	57761	10	66	18
RALI3	66201	9	63	15
JUNLP1	38736	3	11	4
min	7569	9	63	15
median	29172	41	70	48
mean	33118	45	71	48
max	66201	87	83	79
stddev	24062	34	7	30

Table 3: Evaluation of fr-en runs (n_gold=9,043)

(Azpeitia et al., 2017) by which they optimized

VIC1 for F1-score, VIC2 for precision, and VIC3 for recall; the results for German also display the same pattern. The three runs RALI2, RALI1 and RALI3 produce an increasing number of candidate pairs, resulting in a decrease in precision; this leads to an increase in recall only for RALI1, but always to a decrease in F1-score. Reasons for the lower precisions and (to a lesser extent) recalls of the RALI results are proposed in (Grégoire and Langlais, 2017), including the handling of numbers (improved in their later experiments) and the selection of negative training examples.

Only one team submitted runs on the German-English (de-en) language pair, therefore we do not report min, max and other statistics. The results are displayed in Table 4. The precisions and

run_name	sys_n	P (%)	R (%)	F1 (%)
VIC1.de-en	8640	88	80	**84**
VIC3.de-en	9949	82	**85**	**84**
VIC2.de-en	7586	**92**	73	82

Table 4: Evaluation of de-en runs (n_gold=9,550)

F1-scores obtained by VIC for German-English are higher than those they obtained for French-English, with similar recalls. The only difference in the two corpora in terms of statistics is that the German-English dataset was more balanced in its numbers of monolingual sentences, but other differences linked to the intrinsic properties of German and French or to the resources used to train the system for these two languages are likely to have an effect too.

One team submitted runs on the Chinese-English (zh-en) language pair, therefore we do not report min, max and other statistics. The results are displayed in Table 5. According to (Zhang and

run_name	sys_n	P (%)	R (%)	F1 (%)
zNLP1	1985	42	**44**	**43**
zNLP3	1526	**46**	37	41
zNLP2	1900	19	19	19

Table 5: Evaluation of zh-en runs (n_gold=1,896)

Zweigenbaum, 2017), zNLP3 was optimized for precision: this is confirmed by its results on the test set. Overall, the results are lower than the best runs on the fr-en and de-en datasets. Various hypotheses can be proposed to account for this difference, including the different types and sizes of the resources used for translation in VIC and zNLP,

the specific methods used in the two systems, and differences in intrinsic language properties.

5.2 Complementary human evaluation

Were we to know which 'natural' translation pairs existed in the test datasets beyond the translation pairs we inserted, would the results be very different? We did not have resources to perform an extensive human evaluation to answer this question, therefore we designed a minimal experiment on the French-English language pair.

In the VIC and RALI runs, we selected the run with the best precision and randomly drew 20-pair samples. A French native speaker with good command of English examined each sample and scored it according to the grades used in the SemEval 2016 cross-language sentence similarity task (Agirre et al., 2016): (5) The two sentences are completely equivalent, as they mean the same thing; (4) The two sentences are mostly equivalent, but some unimportant details differ; (3) The two sentences are roughly equivalent, but some important information differs or is missing; (2) The two sentences are not equivalent, but share some details; (1) The two sentences are not equivalent, but are on the same topic; (0) The two sentences are on different topics. To check agreement, the first two 20-pair samples were scored by a second French native speaker. Besides, in a few situations, the first judge was sometimes unsure whether to give a score or the next higher score. In these situations, he entered two alternate scores: this created a second series of judgments which differed only in a few places. Altogether, five batches were examined: three for VIC and two for RALI, and for each batch, we had two series of judgments.

For VIC, we sampled 60 sentence pairs from the 978 false positives of the most precise run, Run 2. Out of these sentence pairs, 3–5 were considered as perfect translations (grade 5) and an additional 8–13 were judged as near-perfect translations (grade 4).

From this we computed four increasingly lenient evaluations based upon the minimum and maximum numbers of perfect translations (*5 min, 5 max*) and upon the minimum and maximum numbers of perfect or near-perfect translations (*4–5 min, 4–5 max*). We converted these counts into percentages of the examined false positives that were judged as true translations (*T%FP*). We then extrapolated these percentages to the whole set of false positives to obtain the number of human-judged true positives that should be added to the automatically evaluated true positives (+*TP*). We used this additional number to recompute the true positives and the associated precision (*P'*). Recall cannot be recomputed this way, because to estimate the recall for both automatic and 'natural' translation pairs, we would need to draw a sample from the full test corpus, and given the low prevalence of 'natural' translation pairs, this sample should be quite large. Table 6 shows the corre-

Evaluation	T%FP	+TP	P' (%)	F1' (%)
base (auto)	0.0	0	87.1	79.4
5 (min)	5.0	49	87.7	79.6
5 (max)	8.3	82	88.2	79.8
4–5 (min)	18.3	179	89.4	80.3
4–5 (max)	30.0	293	91.0	80.9

Table 6: Re-evaluation of precision for VIC's Run 2. 'T%FP' is the percentage of human-assessed good translations in the false positives.

sponding evolution of precision. For information we also recomputed the F1-score (*F1'*, still without changing the recall). We observe that precision is reevaluated with an increase of up to 4pt, whereas F1-score gains up to 1.5pt. This difference cannot be ignored for a precise evaluation, but does not bring drastic changes to the overall conclusions of the shared task.

For RALI, we sampled 40 sentence pairs from the 41,865 false positives of the most precise run, Run 2. Out of these sentence pairs, none was considered as perfect translations nor near-perfect translations (most were related though). This is consistent with the fact that RALI2's precision was seven times lower than that of VIC2: a much larger sample might be needed to evidence 'natural' translation pairs in RALI2's output.

This limited experiment suggests that 'natural' translation pairs are much less frequent in the French-English test set than our artificially inserted translation pairs (or that the VIC2 system is much better at spotting the inserted translation pairs than 'natural' translation pairs): Table 6 shows that out of 7569 sentence pairs proposed by VIC2, 87% were inserted translation pairs and between 0.6% and 4% were 'natural' translation pairs. This would extrapolate to a rate of less than 5% of 'natural' translation pairs among the total translation pairs in the corpus.

An important limitation of this experiment is that it examined only a limited sample of sentence pairs, which entails large confidence intervals around the reported values. To compute these confidence intervals, we would need to know more or to make hypotheses about the distribution of 'natural' translation pairs not only in the system-returned sets of sentence pairs, but also outside these sets, which would require more time.

6 Conclusion

We presented the design and results of the second BUCC 2017 Shared Task, which consisted in spotting parallel sentences in comparable corpora. Some participants proposed creative methods, and the best results are quite high, with precisions, recalls and F1-scores between 80% and 88% depending on the language pair. The participants' papers contain directions for further improvement of their methods and results.

To alleviate the need for costly human evaluation, we designed a dataset in which known parallel sentence pairs have been inserted into monolingual corpora. Two risks were associated with this strategy. First, some participants might have tried to 'game' the task by attempting to discover the inserted sentences, for instance using plagiarism detection methods; we are glad that no participant seems to have done so. Second, whereas we could control the inserted translation pairs and try to reduce the likelihood of occurrence of 'natural' translation pairs, we could not fully prevent some from occurring; human examination of sample results from the best runs suggests that 'natural' translation pairs add only a few percents to the inserted translation pairs, confirming the overall relevance of the BUCC 2017 Shared Task dataset and evaluation.

The BUCC 2017 Shared Task dataset and evaluation program can be downloaded from the shared task's Web page.[5]

Acknowledgments

We thank the participants for the time they invested in this task and Léonard Zweigenbaum for his help in assessing the French-English translations. This work was partially funded by the European Union's Horizon 2020 Marie Sklodowska

[5] https://comparable.limsi.fr/bucc2017/bucc2017-task.html.

Curie Innovative Training Networks—European Joint doctorate (ITN-EJD) Under grant agreement No:676207 (MiRoR). Part of this work was supported by a Marie Curie Career Integration Grant within the 7th European Community Framework Programme.

References

Sadaf Abdul-Rauf and Holger Schwenk. 2009. Exploiting comparable corpora with TER and TERp. In *Proceedings of the 2nd Workshop on Building and Using Comparable Corpora: From Parallel to Non-parallel Corpora*. Association for Computational Linguistics, Stroudsburg, PA, USA, BUCC '09, pages 46–54. http://dl.acm.org/citation.cfm?id=1690339.1690351.

Eneko Agirre, Carmen Banea, Daniel Cer, Mona Diab, Aitor Gonzalez-Agirre, Rada Mihalcea, German Rigau, and Janyce Wiebe. 2016. SemEval-2016 Task 1: Semantic textual similarity, monolingual and cross-lingual evaluation. In *Proceedings of the 10th International Workshop on Semantic Evaluation (SemEval-2016)*. Association for Computational Linguistics, San Diego, California, pages 497–511. http://www.aclweb.org/anthology/S16-1081.

Andoni Azpeitia, Thierry Etchegoyhen, and Eva Martínez Garcia. 2017. Weighted set-theoretic alignment of comparable sentences. In *Proceedings of the 10th Workshop on Building and Using Comparable Corpora*. Association for Computational Linguistics, Vancouver, Canada, pages 46–50. http://www.aclweb.org/anthology/W17/W17-1009.

Christian Buck and Philipp Koehn. 2016. Findings of the WMT 2016 bilingual document alignment shared task. In *Proceedings of the First Conference on Machine Translation*. Association for Computational Linguistics, Berlin, Germany, pages 554–563. http://www.aclweb.org/anthology/W16-2347.

Thierry Etchegoyhen and Andoni Azpeitia. 2016. Set-theoretic alignment for comparable corpora. In *Proceedings of the 54th Annual Meeting of the Association for Computational Linguistics (Volume 1: Long Papers)*. Association for Computational Linguistics, Berlin, Germany, pages 2009–2018. http://www.aclweb.org/anthology/P16-1189.

Stephan Gouws, Yoshua Bengio, and Greg Corrado. 2015. BilBOWA: Fast bilingual distributed representations without word alignments. In Francis Bach and David Blei, editors, *Proceedings of the 32nd International Conference on Machine Learning*. Lille, France, volume 37 of *JMLR Workshop and Conference Proceedings*.

Francis Grégoire and Philippe Langlais. 2017. BUCC 2017 Shared Task: a first attempt toward a deep learning framework for identifying parallel sentences in comparable corpora. In *Proceedings of the 10th Workshop on Building and Using Comparable Corpora*. Association for Computational Linguistics, Vancouver, Canada, pages 51–55. http://www.aclweb.org/anthology/W/W17/W17-1010.

Sainik Mahata, Dipankar Das, and Sivaji Bandyopadhyay. 2017. BUCC2017: A hybrid approach for identifying parallel sentences in comparable corpora. In *Proceedings of the 10th Workshop on Building and Using Comparable Corpora*. Association for Computational Linguistics, Vancouver, Canada, pages 61–64. http://www.aclweb.org/anthology/W/W17/W17-1012.

Dragos Stefan Munteanu, Alexander Fraser, and Daniel Marcu. 2004. Improved machine translation performance via parallel sentence extraction from comparable corpora. In Daniel Marcu Susan Dumais and Salim Roukos, editors, *HLT-NAACL 2004: Main Proceedings*. Association for Computational Linguistics, Boston, Massachusetts, USA, pages 265–272.

Martin Potthast, Tim Gollub, Matthias Hagen, Johannes Kiesel, Maximilian Michel, Arnd Oberländer, Martin Tippmann, Alberto Barrón-Cedeño, Parth Gupta, Paolo Rosso, and Benno Stein. 2012. Overview of the 4th international competition on plagiarism detection. In Pamela Forner, Jussi Karlgren, and Christa Womser-Hacker, editors, *CLEF 2012 Evaluation Labs and Workshop, Online Working Notes, Rome, Italy, September 17-20, 2012*. CEUR-WS.org, volume 1178 of *CEUR Workshop Proceedings*. http://ceur-ws.org/Vol-1178/CLEF2012wn-PAN-PotthastEt2012.pdf.

Serge Sharoff, Pierre Zweigenbaum, and Reinhard Rapp. 2015. BUCC shared task: Cross-language document similarity. In *Proceedings of the Eighth Workshop on Building and Using Comparable Corpora*. Association for Computational Linguistics, Beijing, China, pages 74–78.

Masao Utiyama and Hitoshi Isahara. 2003. Reliable measures for aligning japanese-english news articles and sentences. In *Proceedings of the 41st Annual Meeting of the Association for Computational Linguistics*. Association for Computational Linguistics, Sapporo, Japan, pages 72–79. https://doi.org/10.3115/1075096.1075106.

Zheng Zhang and Pierre Zweigenbaum. 2017. zNLP: Identifying parallel sentences in Chinese-English comparable corpora. In *Proceedings of the 10th Workshop on Building and Using Comparable Corpora*. Association for Computational Linguistics, Vancouver, Canada, pages 56–60. http://www.aclweb.org/anthology/W/W17/W17-1011.

Pierre Zweigenbaum, Serge Sharoff, and Reinhard
Rapp. 2016. Towards preparation of the second
BUCC shared task: Detecting parallel sentences in
comparable corpora. In *Proceedings of the Ninth
Workshop on Building and Using Comparable
Corpora*. European Language Resources Association (ELRA), Portorož, Slovenia, pages 38–43.
https://comparable.limsi.fr/bucc2016/pdf/BUCC08.pdf.

Author Index

Association for Computational Linguistics
209 N. Eighth Street
Stroudsburg, Pennsylvania 18360

ISBN 978-1-5108-4575-6